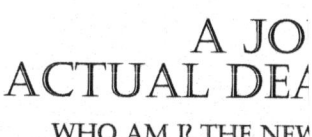

An Exploration of the Human Consciousness
through Spiritual Intervention

SCIENCE AND SPIRITUALITY COMBINED

Beverley J. Gilmour

Also by Beverley Gilmour

Children's Title -
Island of Ice and the Snowmites [*Gilmory James*]

# About the Author

Beverley Gilmour has lived with chronic Actual Death Experiences since 1987. They occur frequently, often as many as three to four times a month. She is the only known medical case in the world to be currently treated by the medical sector for this chronic condition, for which she is also registered disabled.

In 1993, Beverley began compiling extensive and controversial Spiritual Writings detailing her ADEs and in 2017, she will be launching the Human Consciousness Scientific Observational Universal Learning [SOUL] Project, to change the way the scientific world understands the Actual Death Experience.

In 2014, Beverley graduated from The University of Central Lancashire after studying an honours degree in Film, Television and Screenwriting. In September 2017, she will be returning to the University to study for her Ph.D in Psychology.

Beverley began her writing career as a Children's Author in 1986, creating a series of fantasy characters, 'The Snowmites,' and she secured a publishing deal in 1991. Inspired by experiencing many encounters with the Spirit of the late Walt Disney during her Actual Death Experiences, Beverley re-vamped her characters and storylines and her first book, Island of Ice and the Snowmites was published in 2009. She now spends her time writing screenplays inspired by her Actual Death Experiences, and she holds private consultations to help people understand the ADE. She is also involved in giving public presentations on Actual Death Experiences.

Her true life story delivers a message of hope and understanding both for the future of mankind, and for the existence of the New Earth and New Heaven, and gives the answer to the most philosophical and universal question ever asked about the concept of human immortality: "Is there an Afterlife?"

Her words are as inspiring as they are frightening. Now for the very first time, she opens her heart and her life to share with the world her graphic accounts of both life and death.

# *Thoughts*

*What are these thoughts that surround me?*
*The visions that dance through my head.*
*Let me show you the world, I encounter*
*When I am alone in my bed.*
*Break - free from this life that enchains me*
*From thoes oblivious to my Soul.*
*Break - free, and ride a cloud into the night.*
*And to my friend, my Spirit I behold.*


*"Observe and take notice of thy self"*

Merlin Book Publishers [UK]
4A Station Road  Lytham  Lancashire.  FY85DH. ENGLAND.

This edition first published in the UK in 2016 by Merlin Books. A subsidiary company of The Merlin Corporation Limited. Established since 1987.

Design and typography © Beverley Gilmour

Text © Beverley Gilmour 2016

All rights reserved.
No part of this publication may be reproduced, stored in a retrieval system, or transmitted in any form, or by any means, electrical, mechanical, photocopying, recording or otherwise without prior written permission of The Merlin Corporation Limited Registered Company Number 4324374 or a license permitting restricted copying. Worldwide such licenses are granted by The Merlin Corporation Limited [UK].

# Acknowledgements

I would like to acknowledge and thank my two sons Oliver and Westley-John, whose trust and support over the years has been immeasurable; their love - infinite... I would also like to thank my General Practitioner, Dr Jenny Franklin whose exceptional professionalism and consideration gave me the strength to continue seeking the answers... My Psychologist, Mr. Roger Rowlands whose *'love of laughter'* helped me to find the humour again... Dr Neil Curzon, whose individuality and protection gave me the confidence to have faith in the medical sector again... Dr. Best, who from the onset taught me to *'hold on tight'* as it was going to be an extremely difficult road ahead for me... Dr. Penny Sartori Ph.D, RGN, author of *'The Wisdom of Near-Death Experiences: How Understanding NDE's Can Help Us Live More Fully.'* Her own Study of the NDE was a meeting of two minds... And to Susan Mears, my Literary Agent. Her guidance and support inspired me to write this book... And to Julian Robbins, Editor and Story Advisor... To all my Tutors, Disability Student Support, and my personal Note-Takers at the University of Central Lancashire, who organised a network of support that permitted me to study for my degree... To Amanda Stable for her proof reading... Amanda Chapman, Susan Goodwin, Kym Warham and Lorraine Keady, my four most dearest and cherished friends...

And to my loving Mother, Rene Joyce Potts whose own love gave me life...

# Dedication
## To
Kieran O'Mahoney, Richard Hargrieves,
John Turner and Francis-John Murphy

*Never Forgotten*

# Contents

Introduction     5

1] The Actual Death Experience     15
2] Are You My Lord Jesus?     28
3] The Relationship of Consciousness:
Between The Physical Mind and The Spiritual Mind.     40
4] The Controversial Enlightenment     53
5] Forgiveness     74
6] The Dancing Demons     90
7] Paradise     106
8] Living With Chronic Actual-Death Experiences:
Part One     120
9] Living With Chronic Actual-Death Experiences:
Part Two     143
10] The Fairytale     164

11] Conclusion     184

Appendix     197
References     213

Book Reviews     214

## Actual-Death Experiences

| | |
|---|---|
| 1] Are You My Lord Jesus? | 28 |
| 2] Around the Earth in its Global Form. | 32 |
| 3] The Marble Steps | 35 |
| | |
| 4] Before Him We Shall Sit. | 54 |
| 5] Is This Your Paradise? | 60 |
| 6] Learn To Do As You Are Told Beverley. | 63 |
| 7] The Swear Word is Muted in Heaven. | 68 |
| | |
| 8] I am Sorry About Your Mother | 78 |
| 9] Go Into The Light. | 82 |
| 10] Cleansing The Spirit. | 85 |
| | |
| 11] Speak The Lord's Prayer. | 91 |
| 12] The Invisible Shield. | 92 |
| 13] The Dancing Demons of the Evil Mind. | 94 |
| 14] The Birth of His Spirit | 98 |
| 15] Swallowed By The Mouth of Darkness. | 101 |
| | |
| 16] Central Park - New York. | 110 |
| 17] The Bumble Bees Do Not Sting Here. | 113 |
| 18] Leave Me Of Your Company. | 115 |
| 19] Have You Heard of Nostradamus? | 116 |

## Actual-Death Experiences

20] Where Is My Baby? 123
21] This Woman is Pregnant 135
22] The Birth of the Child in the Spirit 139

23] Teach Me Your Magic:
   The Spirit of the Late Walt Disney. 168

## Author's Note

Some names of the people in this book
have been change to protect their identity

# Introduction

Our world today is one of constant chaos and controlled instability. Of economic fever induced by financial deterioration accumulating from vast International debts, and humanitarian crises rising up from the ashes of natural disasters, human existence has become conditioned by the laws of survival. The third world illustrates the powerful reality as to how easily the delicate balance between man and nature can be upset beyond healing. Mankind has evolved since the known primitive age of the prehistoric caveman, and has now advanced beyond comprehension. Incredibly, the human species has matured in all aspects of social sophistication with the exception of one - War! The venomous destruction of people and of the land. Is there any hope left for peace, or is modern mankind destined to continue making the same mistakes as our ancestors through history?

In being the only known case of a subject of chronic Actual Death Experiences to be currently treated by the medical sector, and registered as disabled for the condition, I now put pen to paper to share with my readers the story of my experiences; both of the physical death, and of the traumatic journey of emotions I was forced to endure for over three decades of my life. How, even now, in our modern 21st century, I've had to fight for my existence. My life as a young woman, a mother of children, and a successful Children's Authoress gone, vanished in a whisper; an identity that disappeared overnight, crushed by a stampede of deceit and professional abuse from the British Justice System, I was made homeless. Forced onto the streets to find shelter in the cold, dark, uninviting doorways, my innocent children as babes in my arms were ripped away from my warm, loving, and tender embrace. I was forced to wander the streets without any food, money or my personal belongings.

I lost my right as a woman, and as a young mother. I lost my right to be protected by the British law. I lost my right to exist as a human being. I became a faceless ghost amidst a harrowing reality of man's lack of consciousness for life. I became an existence without a voice.

Why did this happen to me? Why did I suddenly find myself living in the shadows of life? Why had my reality so suddenly become a festering world of judgement and abandonment?

It happened simply because I was considered different. I am a disabled person with a rare coma-induced medical condition, 'chronic Actual Death Experiences', [aka Near-Death Experiences - NDEs]: a medical condition that is able to help us to understand more fully the human consciousness and what happens to us when we die; a rare insight into the structure of the human mind, and a source of explanation for how the human Spirit governs all our emotions; for the first time in all known scientific investigations, a medical condition that whilst under medical supervision can give the answer to the most philosophical and universal question ever asked about the concept of human immortality: "Is there an Afterlife?"

## Introduction

When I first embarked upon writing this book, I wanted to ensure my written words would make a difference to people's lives. In sharing my story, I hope to raise greater awareness for the concept of human life, and a real understanding of the physical aspect of the Actual Death Experience. Although I have claimed to be the only known medical case being currently treated for chronic Actual Death Experiences, I do not rule out the possibility that there are other people in the world who also have this condition, whether they are currently receiving treatment for it or not. In raising awareness for the chronic Actual Death Experience, we may actually identify other individuals to whom this might also be happening.

However, in general terms, it does not matter if an individual has only had one Actual Death Experience or several. It does not matter if their experience or experiences were recent or twenty years ago. The ADE is such a profound psychological event that a subject need have only one to turn their world upside down. An individual's entire persona is often changed after the ADE. Usually, afterwards, they will no longer have any feelings of fear towards death itself. In being given confirmation that life exists after the physical death, they will normally expand their belief psyche to absorb the reality of life's much greater purpose, and most who experience ADE will tell you they feel as if they have undergone a Spiritual awakening.

Although the ADE subject may no longer fear death or the process of dying, there is still one fear that remains engraved within their thoughts: the fear of rejection by their friends and loved ones. The fear of not being believed, or being considered mentally unwell by those they care about, forces them to keep silent about their ADE. In raising awareness of the Actual Death Experience, I hope to erase that fear of rejection, and help the ADE subject to realise that having an ADE is nothing to be ashamed of. Hopefully, this book will help to encourage every ADE subject to talk openly with anyone about their Actual Death Experience.

The reality of my own physical life shattered my heart into a million pieces. I was an ADE subject burdened with the fear of rejection, and as my ADEs over the years were of constant occurrence, I developed a self-doubt that created a suppressed emotion of sadness. I was learning the most incredible knowledge, frequently witnessing a wonder of astonishing sights; but more importantly, I was encountering Jesus in every single Actual Death Experience. I was on a phenomenal journey of Spiritual awakening, but I was never able to find an inner peace of acceptance for my ADEs.

I struggled every day with a sense of desperation at believing I was different from other people. The seeds of anxiety were sown so deep within my sadness that I was blinded, unable to recognise the miraculous truth of being with Jesus. I lacked self-confidence and just wanted my ADEs to stop, but they never did. No one knew the truth behind my smile. Inside I was crying - yearning for peace.

I cradled the flickering light of my irregular heartbeat and nursed it into a strength, devoting my entire life to my children, and to my writing career. Then on the threshold of success, I fell victim to gossip and accusation; the pointed finger, the label of insanity. Jealousy had reared its ugly head and destruction was its well-prepared feast. It all happened so fast, one day I had the world at my feet, the next reality I knew, I was in the gutter.

Although I never spoke freely about my Actual Death Experiences, I did mention them in passing to close friends and family. I never spoke about meeting with Jesus, but I didn't need to. My fate was already sealed by the mere fact that other people thought I was different, and I literally became too afraid to reveal I was being carried away in the Spirit by Jesus.

I spent the best part of the following twenty-three years just trying to find someone to help me. Someone who could help me cultivate the knowledge Jesus was teaching me. Someone who would help me to regain my physical life as the woman, the mother, and as the successful Children's Authoress. I wanted to help people to find peace in their fears of the physical death, and to know with certainty that it is not the end. To teach people they have no reason to be afraid of death, as the natural physical death is not a painful process, but rather it is a simple and most beautiful transition of consciousness. I wanted to give people a truth to celebrate, in the knowledge that mankind will indeed survive, and continue to exist in a world of peace and human evolution. In a world where war and destruction, famine and disease are nothing more than a memory lost in the shadows of time.

I have walked upon the New Earth in my Actual Death Experiences. Witnessed a beauty that will strike the heart of man with more force than a bolt of lighting. I have written this book for all the reasons given in this introduction, and also because I want people to rejoice in the knowledge that one day they will be reunited with their loved ones who have already passed over into the Afterlife. I want to help people to dry their eyes from their tears of loss, and to teach people how to heal their broken hearts. To reveal Spiritual teachings that will free people from social and spiritual domination, and enrich their physical lives beyond recognition.

I searched in vain for years to meet an individual who could help me bring together the knowledge I have been given through my Actual Death Experiences. In March 2015, my search finally came to an end when by a guided trust, I encountered my literary Agent, Susan Mears. On hearing my life-story she knew exactly what was needed to bring the Spiritual awakening out into the public domain. I needed to write this book. I needed to tell my story from the heart of a woman and a mother of children, so that everyone would come to realise that regardless of my medical condition and disability, I am truly no different from anyone else. I do have a right to a life, and Susan proved to me I do also have a voice. In this book, therefore, I reveal the true origin of the Spiritual teachings.

Although it is my life story, the one behind the knowledge is Jesus. In every single Actual Death Experience I have had since 1987, Jesus is the one whom I meet with in the Spirit. He is always there waiting for me to pass over into the Afterlife, and then in this heavenly existence I begin a journey with him in which he is my teacher. He is the one who mended my broken heart, and aspects of my journey with him is portrayed within the Book of Revelation.

## Introduction

For the first five years of my Actual Death Experiences, I did not write anything down about them. Then on a daily basis from 1993 to 1996, I compiled pages and pages of hand-written accounts describing them, and explaining the teachings behind them. I refer to these pages as the 'Who Am I?' Spiritual Prophecies of Jesus. My aim has been to share with readers an understanding both of these, and the medical aspect of my ADEs. In Jesus's 'Who Am I?' Spiritual Prophecies there are elements of essential scientific importance, with an equally primary Spiritual foundation. The union of the two is the core for a new Spiritual Awareness in modern 'Science and Spirituality Combined'.

In this book I have also discussed how, within our physical lives, we have an influential relationship with our own Spirit, [*The Relationship of Consciousness*]. This chapter explores how your existence within the Afterlife depends upon how you nurture this relationship during your physical life. I have also focused on how learning to prepare ourselves for the physical death can actually '*free*' us of all negativity, and unhealthy social and emotional forms of suppression. In understanding your Spiritual existence now, you can transform your physical life to create a happy, stress-free, peaceful life and generate the self-confidence to succeed in both your personal and your business endeavours, whilst at the same time teaching yourself to become of a beautiful Spirit in preparation for when you pass over into your eternal life.

In bringing the Actual Death Experience into the mindset of individuals who have not had an ADE, we can learn to combine Science and Spirituality to lay down the foundations for a future society no longer scarred by the rule of violence and war. The Spirit, while still within the physical body, communicates by means of telepathy. In the *'Who Am I?'* Prophecies of Jesus, He teaches us how to cultivate our telepathic source, so we may begin our next stage of human evolution.

Imagine a world in which we are able to communicate with one another by means of telepathy! War would become absolved. State Leaders and Soldiers alike would be able to communicate with one another directly to resolve issues of dispute. Crime Rates would plummet as criminals acknowledged there is no longer the reality of an unsuspecting victim. In understanding our Spirit now, the ability to make great changes is our reward.

After the publication of this book, I intend to launch the Human Consciousness Scientific Observational Universal Learning [SOUL] Project. My intent is to create a global *'Collective Consciousness'* for the Actual Death Experience in the combination of Science and Spirituality. The HC-Soul Project aims to give everyone the opportunity to ask questions and seek the answers in the publishing of an *'open debate'* for the collective consciousness. The *'Who Am I?'* Spiritual Prophecies of Jesus teach us that *'The Human Consciousness is the Spiritual Entity of Man'*. Such teaching changes everything we thought we knew in our scientific understanding of the consciousness.

The HC-Soul Project will also follow the research findings of a planned revolutionary scientific investigation, in which a *'link'* between Human DNA and the Actual Death Experience might be established. The aim is to determine if there is a *'common component'* in the DNA of individuals who have experienced an Actual Death Experience, which is not present in people who have not.

The most voiced scientific argument surrounding ADEs is to question the probability as to: *'How is it possible for a person to come back to life after their heart has stopped and their brain is no longer producing any activity?'* [*especially in cases where the individual has been flatlined for a substantial amount of time*]. The scientific viewpoint is that such a thing should not be possible, as once the brain has ceased to function and our organs have shut down, the cells in our physical body deteriorate rapidly.

In the reality of living with chronic Actual Death Experiences for the past twenty-eight years, I believe the answer is within our DNA. The hypothesis being that we will be able to establish a common component in the DNA of individuals who have experienced ADE, and it is their genetic code that *'preserves the human cells'* for a longer period of time after the physical body has shut down and the physical death has been established. If this hypothesis is endorsed by scientific investigation, we will be looking at possible *'new cures'* for all illnesses related to cell deterioration simply by the transferring of human DNA.

*A Hungry Man*

*On the first day*
*Should a hungry man come to you*
*Give him food.*

*On the second day*
*Should he come again*
*Hungry as the day before*
*Give him food.*

*On the third day*
*Should he return*
*Hungry still...*
*Teach this man to fish.*

*Never turn away from a hungry man.*
*For the day may come*
*when it is you in need of food.*

# 1

## The Actual Death Experience

Most readers will be more familiar with the term Near Death Experience (NDE). The Actual Death Experience is the same phenomenon as the NDE, and it has all the same characteristics as an NDE. However, the phrase Actual Death Experience has been given to the phenomenon to help define it more clearly from a scientific point of view. The phenomenon can actually be historically traced as far back as *Plato's Republic* (380 B.C), and it is featured in the pages of the Bible: *Paul's Vision and His Thorn in the Flesh* (2 Corinthians 12: 1-9), and in the account given by *John the Apostle in the book of Revelation The New Jerusalem* (Rev 21: 10).

It was not until 1975 that the public's interest in the phenomenon truly peaked, after Dr Raymond Moody Ph.D., Ms.D., a prominent scholar and lecturer, published his first of many books, *Life After Life*, in which he coined the phrase 'Near Death Experience'. *Life After Life* sold over thirteen million copies world-wide, and it was later turned into a feature film. Dr Moody defined the NDE as an experience undergone while unconscious, occurring close to death, in which the individual then reports experiencing a series of events taking place which cannot be accredited to the physical world. Moody currently continues to investigate the phenomenon, and he is recognized as one of the leading authorities on the subject.

However, in more recent times as a result of the scientific world taking an interest in the phenomenon, Moody's definition has generated a conflict of understanding, and had lead to ongoing debates. In particular, Dr Sam Parnia M.D., Ph.D., M.R.C.P., who also refers to the phenomenon as an Actual Death Experience rather than an NDE, has publicly stated that the reason for his variance comes from the scientific view of physical death. Parnia explained:

*"We define death when there is no heartbeat, no breathing, and the brain is no longer functioning. When a patient has died and has all the vital signs of death, he or she is no longer alive. It is a clear scientific finding - the patient is either dead or alive. It is scientifically impossible to be of both at the precise same time as the other, which is what the term Near Death suggests. We have scientifically proven it is possible to bring a patient back after death has been established, which clearly indicates the patient has had an Actual Death Experience and not a Near Death Experience."*

Dr Sam Parnia has worked extensively in the study of death and Human Consciousness. He is currently the Assistant Professor of Critical Care Medicine at the Stony Brook Medical Centre in New York. Parnia also launched the *AWARE* (AWAreness during REsuscitation) study through the *Human Consciousness Project,* and he is currently the Chairman and Trustee of *The Horizon Research Foundation.* He has published in leading scientific and medical peer-reviewed journals, and is also the author of two popular science books, *Erasing Death: The Science That Is Rewriting the Boundaries Between Life and*

*Death* (2013) and *What Happens When We Die?* (2006), and five other titles. His work has also featured in many newspapers and magazines all over the world including the *Guardian, Telegraph, GQ, Psychology Today, Time, Newsweek,* as well as on the BBC and CNN.

### Characteristics of the Actual Death Experience

*The Tunnel - Darkness and Light:* Although not every ADE subject reports seeing a tunnel of light, it is still one of the most common characteristics of the Actual Death Experience. After passing over into the Spirit, subjects find themselves surrounded by a darkness, and in the distance they can see a bright glowing light towards which they sense themselves being drawn. Then as they get nearer to the light it becomes brighter. Some subjects will report seeing the shadow of a figure or several figures within the light, who appear to be waiting for them to enter into it. In other reports subjects can sometimes know instinctively not to go towards the light, as they will not be able to return to their physical body if they do, and so they will attempt to pull themselves back away from it.

*Encountering A Deceased Loved One:* This is another common characteristic of the Actual Death Experience, and for many people probably the most profound, which continues to have a deep effect on the subject after the ADE is over. Individuals often report that a shadowy figure they saw waiting within the bright light turns out to be a loved one who has already passed over. Often they recognize the loved one before any communication has been exchanged between them both; even if their loved one has dramatically changed in appearance. They may now look much younger than the subject remembers.

When a subject meets a loved one it is usually to be given a message. Sometimes they are told to *Go back, as it is not your time to be here yet.*

The message given by a loved one always seems to have importance. In some cases subjects may just be told by their loved one that they are at peace now and happy, and that they are not to worry about them.

*Life Review:* The Life Review component in an Actual Death Experience is not a common characteristic that appears in ADEs, but it is a very prominent feature, and it tends to have a significant reason for its presence. The ADE is complex and usually only understood by the actual subjects, who will find themselves viewing events that have occurred within their physical lives through what appears to be three-dimensional perception. As the image and scenes flash in front of them, they feel an emotional attachment associated with the scene. They may feel regret and sadness on being shown a situation in which they had behaved badly, or were wrong in how they had handled things. The life review ADE is always an experience of the *learning of a truth* that the subject hadn't realised or understood. Once the ADE is over, the subject will usually correct his or her past mistakes or make changes to his or her physical life to ensure such mistakes are not repeated.

*Telepathic Communications and Unity:* The ability to communicate within an ADE (and therefore within the Afterlife) is recognized as an exchange of *telepathic thoughts* rather than actual verbal conversation. This explains the *feelings* most ADE subjects have when they report sensing a feeling of being connected to others

## The Actual Death Experience

around them, even though they cannot actually see anyone else nearby. Other ADE subjects will report feeling as if they have developed a heightened sense of awareness, becoming tuned into the universe.

*Visions of the Future:* Many ADE subjects will describe being shown a future event that will occur within their physical lives or in the life of someone they know. Usually these type of ADEs are difficult to identify any explanation for, as the subject does not always realise at the time of being shown the vision that it is actually a future event. Most ADE subjects will only make the connection after the event has occurred, which suggests the vision was given without any real purpose. However, I believe visions of the future do have a very valuable objective. If a subject wrote down a description of the vision, signed and dated the text (witnessed), then sealed it into an envelope and put it away in a safe place, the text could be retrieved after the event has happened and this would lead to confirmation that the information given during an ADE was from a spiritual source.

There are many more characteristics to the ADE. The most common of them all is when a subject describes being surrounded by an incredible feeling of 'love' and sensing a 'peacefulness' that is difficult for them to describe, as it was so strong it overwhelmed their senses. ADE subjects also describe finding themselves in the most beautiful landscape surrounded by gardens of intense beauty and colour, and being able to see buildings, which actually appear to emit a presence of life. It is understandable that due to the many different ADE variations that subjects report, - the science world has had a difficult time identifying the ADE. Unlike the physical process of death, which occurs as a series of events in an identical sequence regardless of the individual; the actual ADE, (*the experience of death itself*) is a process of Human Consciousness. No two ADE's will be identical for two individuals, as no two people are exactly the same in all their speech, mannerisms and thoughts. The common characteristics of the Actual Death Experience do however establish without doubt that 'another world' other than the physical world exists, and that our 'life form' continues to exist after the physical body has stopped functioning.

### What Happens to Us When We Die?

The physical death is a painless process. It is a peaceful and a very beautiful transition. If you are a person who fears death or the thought of dying, I do hope you will be able to find some comfort in my words. Naturally, when I say death is painless, I am referring to the 'natural death' in this instance. The process of the physical death advances in a *sequence of stages*; death does not transpire in just *one single moment,* as once believed by the majority mindset. It is an exceptional peaceful and very beautiful process in a tranquil passing of consciousness, in which we maintain the complete awareness during its progression.

When I have an Actual Death experience, the first recognition I always have is in the acknowledgement of a change occurring around the inside area of my head. It feels like a sudden wave is flowing around inside my head, similar to the sensation you can feel just as you are drifting off to sleep. It is more intense but not painful. I

## The Actual Death Experience

know I am going to have an Actual Death Experience as I can feel myself going down, down, down - deeper and deeper into myself. This is the stages of unconsciousness.

The awareness I feel at this stage is a sense that I am *actually awake*. I can hear and see everything that is going on in the room around me but I am fully aware my eyelids are closed, and I am lying down upon my bed. I can hear my own thoughts commanding, *Wake up, wake up!* but I can never follow through on the command.

As the level of unconsciousness deepens, I become aware of a change in my heartbeat. It becomes faint and I sense my heartbeat slowing down. Then my breathing starts to change. I have a shortness of breath and my breathing becomes shallow. At this point I sense the area of my throat becoming tight, as if it is closing upon itself. I feel the need to swallow in an attempt to force a breath but I can't inhale properly, and I can hear my shallow breathing making a crackling sound. This sound is known as the *death rattle*.

Individuals who have witnessed my condition as I begin the Actual Death experience always notice *I become unresponsive, my lips have turned blue, I have no pulse and they hear the death rattle*. The final stage of change before the actual separation, the *physical death - passing over*, is within my brain. I begin to feel the sensation that my brain is *shutting down*. It happens very quickly in a consecutive sequence of four different processes, always in the same order. It is as if someone has flipped a switch and the light goes out.

The first part is the top right-hand side of my brain,

followed by the bottom right-hand side; then the top left-hand side, followed by the bottom left hand-side. The best way to describe this part of the process is to imagine yourself slowly dunking yourself under water. As your head submerges - your senses suddenly begins to feel *blocked* and *out of co-ordination.* The moment the last section of my brain has shut down, I feel my consciousness separating, and I begin to rise upwards and out of my physical body. I have now experienced the physical death and passed over into the Spirit - the Afterlife.

When my Spirit returns back into my physical body after the Actual Death Experience has finished, the events that occur are also always in the same order. Firstly, I have the awareness of being back inside my physical body, the same sensation as when my consciousness has separated just before it begins to rise upwards.

The next stage happens very quickly. I focus on the centre back of my brain - the brain-stem. Then I experience a sensation as if I am suddenly hitting a brick wall, thudding against something solid. I sense a loud *bang.* A small ball of electrifying energy of light appears, which then rushes down the inside of my physical body. I sense the ball of energy making direct contact with my heart, striking my heart like an electrifying bolt of lightning.

As this happens my physical body goes into a spasm, jumping upwards in a jerking movement. The ball of energy generated from my brain-stem restarts my heartbeat; similar to when a patient goes into cardiac arrest and an electric shock is used to restore the heart's regular rhythm. I then gasp for breath. Usually it takes only one bolt of electricity to restart my heart, but there have been occasions when my heart has been struck two or three times before I start breathing again.

To explain this process more scientifically, one should consider the process from the perspective of human consciousness. During our sleep mode, our Second Consciousness (the sub-conscious) becomes our Primary Consciousness - changing the brain's main activity from the left hand side to the right hand side.

*Left Hemisphere:*

The left brain is the logical side, responsible for words, reasoning, numbers, analysis, lists and sequences. It controls the right hand side of the body.

*Right Hemisphere:*

The right brain is the creative side, responsible for rhythm, spatial awareness, colour, the imagination, day-dreaming, holistic awareness and dimension. It controls the left hand side of the body.

In my Actual Death Experiences, I by-pass the dream state and reach unconsciousness. This stage causes my heartbeat to change, which then triggers the Second Consciousness (the sub-conscious) to activate my Higher Consciousness (the Spiritual Mind - the Consciousness of God). Then as my Higher Consciousness becomes my Primary Consciousness, my brain begins to shut down. Once the fourth section of my brain has shut down my Higher Consciousness separates from the Second

Consciousness, and I begin to rise upwards and out of my physical body. This is what I mean when I write, *I became of the Spirit,* as I no longer have any connection to my physical body.

When my ADE's first began in 1987, I didn't even know what an Actual Death Experience was, and although I never really spoke openly to other people about my ADEs, I did try to find out why I was having them. In one of the early 1987 ADEs, Jesus took my Spirit to meet with the Spirit of my late father, John Gilmour, (See the ADE *Learn to do as you are told, Beverley*). After this, I began to realise fully that I was experiencing death and passing over into the Afterlife, as my father had died in 1982.

My first thoughts from my realisation were: *I must be cheating death. It must be my time to go but I don't want to die and that is why I keep coming back.* The thought of dying and never seeing my husband David and my baby daughter Samantha, or my family and my friends again terrified me. It terrified my every waking moment for months, until eventually I couldn't cope any longer without knowing the reason for why I was having these experiences.

At the time, I believed if I could just find out why I was having them, then maybe I could control them, and then stop them happening to me. I turned to my dear friend Susan Goodwin and found the courage to confide in her. Susan's response shocked me, but it also gave me a glimmer of hope:

"You're having those Out of Body Experiences. I

saw a programme about them the other day. Don't worry, lots of people have them."

Her words were soothing to my ears: *Don't worry, lots of people have them.* It didn't take me long before I found myself quietly sitting in the audience of a meeting at a local Spiritualist Church. I listened solemnly to people recounting their stories of their Out of Body experiences, (OBEs) and of Near Death Experiences (NDEs).

Although many of the accounts I heard bore similarities to my own experiences (e.g. the tunnel of light, meeting with a dead relative), there wasn't one person who described having constant experiences, and always meeting with Jesus. I left the Church feeling disheartened, but at least I had now learnt about the existence of the Spiritual phenomenon, and that helped to settle my flustered mind.

I soon learnt not everyone was as accepting and open minded as my friend Susan, and in the following years of my Actual Death Experiences, I became reluctant to even tell people about my ADEs. I found most people's first reaction was one of disbelief or of fear. People seemed to jump to the conclusion it was all just 'crazy talk' or they instantly changed the conversation when they realised I was talking about death.

My husband David was no exception, and although we had been together since 1982, his reaction to my revelation I was meeting with Jesus in Actual Death Experiences was so severe - our relationship never fully recovered. David never looked at me again in the same way as he used to. In his eyes, I had suddenly stopped being the wife he loved and the mother of his child. In his eyes, I had become a 'freak of nature' and his opinion remained this way right up until our separation in 1992, and even during and after our divorce four years later.

Most ADE subjects often face the same traumatic experience of not being believed or worse being considered by their friends, loved ones and even the medical profession as being mentally unbalanced. It is a burden that no one should be forced to carry; especially not in our present day society of individuality acceptance. Millions of people all over the world have reported having an Actual Death Experience, yet still, there is often the fear of rejection and not being believed by the ADE subject.

How is it possible a Spiritual phenomenon that is not only featured in the pages of the Bible, but can also be dated back as far as Plato create such a negative response by the non-ADE subject? It has been proven by the science world that an individual can indeed die and then be brought back to life; so why does the individual's account of their death still cause such a conflict of medical opinion?

The answer to solve all academic arguments will not be found in scientific investigations alone. It requires the combination of both science and spirituality. I term spirituality as a person's perception, his or her belief structure - in basic terms the 'human consciousness'.

## *The Consciousness*

*"I am part of something far greater
than the eye can see.
The memories of such however,
remain hidden within me."*

*Who Am I?
I am a Woman and a Mother of Children*

# 2

### Actual-Death Experience
## Are You My Lord Jesus?

I stood gazing around at my surroundings. The mountains of clouds folded into each other, blanketing my view in every direction. I was a lone figure amidst a sanctuary of light. I reached down and trailed my hand through the soft, flowing, velvety white clouds. As my hand gently passed through the smoothness, the clouds scattered in slow motion, floating upwards and drifting along in the air. I was able to make things move here in this world. In a world where I was standing in the Spirit. The existence of life without the physical body. I belonged to this world. I had finally returned home. There was not a sound to be heard. The stillness of silence lingered all around me, yet I knew, I knew I was being touched by the very essence of life itself. Sensing the glorious setting of harmony, I felt at peace here in this world. I did not want to close my eyes upon the beauty before me; not wanting even the darkness of a blink from the flutter of my eyelids to take me away from this spiritual utopia.

Alerting my attention, I caught sight of a small group of people in the distance walking towards me. I could hear them individually speaking to me through the vibrations of their footsteps. I knew only not to concern myself with thoughts questioning their identity, for everything would be revealed to me, and I had nothing to fear. Within moments they were all standing by my side, and they gathered around me in a horseshoe circle. I noticed they were all male, and dressed in long, off-white flowing robes Without any vocal sound being made, I heard one of them say,

*"We are the true disciples of Jesus."*

I remained silent. I understood his words but I was not able to utter a sound.

Suddenly, the sole figure of a man walked out from behind the clouds. He stepped forward and stood directly in front of me. His presence emanated a majestic aura, which bestowed an immense beauty of magnificence. The sudden sense of 'knowing' captured my entire being. Instinctively I knew this man was Jesus, yet still I was unable to say anything.

I became aware of His disciples gently guiding me within my thoughts: *Honour the Son of God.* Immediately I lowered my head to bow respectfully before Him, and finally I was able to speak.

*"Are you my Lord Jesus?"* I heard myself asking Him. I don't know why I had asked Him this question. I knew without any uncertainty He was Jesus. There was no mistaking the ambience I felt in His presence - the purity of an unconditional love, asserting great authority. Then He spoke.

*"Why do you ask, Child, do you not know?"* His tone was commanding, yet also soothing. I fell to my knees,

overwhelmed with remorse. Why had I asked such a foolish question when I knew who He was? Did I truly have so little faith in my own senses?

Jesus placed a large wooden cross in the form of a necklace over my head. The height of the cross touched my knees, and I heard Him say, *"Do not be afraid, Child, for you shall always be protected."*

There I remained upon my knees, surrounded by His disciples, as Jesus turned and walked back into His heavenly paradise. A moment later, I was back in my physical body.

It may actually have been minutes or even hours later. I do not know for certain how long it takes for me to return back into my physical body after an Actual Death Experience. The concept of time seems to have no significance over the events occurring when I am in the Spirit, regardless of whether I am having the Actual Death Experience or I am back in my physical body, and waiting for my heart to start beating again.

The only indication suggesting my Actual Death Experiences are not all of the same duration is in how long it takes for my recovery process to be complete, after the ADE has finished. When I start breathing again and I have regained consciousness, I can't just sit up or get straight out of bed. Sometimes it can take me up to an hour or even several hours before I have the full use of my physical limbs again.

In the midst of trying to reconnect with my physical body, my thoughts are also consumed with filtering the memory of the Actual Death Experience: *Why did I see what I did? What did it mean? Why is this happening to me? Why am I always meeting Jesus?* The questions are endless, and impatience fuels my desire to discover the answers, answers that would take over two decades to be given by Jesus. Jesus - the one who always came and carried my Spirit to walk with Him within the Spirit, to be His Witness for the existence of the New Earth and the New Heaven and the future of mankind.

I was twenty-two years old when my Actual Death experiences began in 1987, and in every ADE I have always encountered Jesus. He just appears when I have passed over into the Afterlife. Most times I see him straight away, but there are other times when I move at such an incredible speed that I don't see him until after I have passed through the bright light.

I would usually have two to three Actual Death Experiences every few weeks, but in the early 90s, by late 1992, my ADEs escalated, occurring as frequently as three to four times a month. In total I've had thousands of ADEs, and every single one of them has had a purpose. During the first five years of my ADEs, I did not write down any notes about what Jesus was showing me within the experience, and I didn't know the reason as to why I was having them. I knew only that Jesus was teaching me about the Spirit, and that under His protection no harm would ever come to me within the Afterlife.

In those early years of my Actual Death Experiences, if anyone had suggested I didn't trust Jesus as much as I believed I did, I suspect I would have responded with anger. I believed I trusted Jesus without any uncertainty, and I would not have taken kindly to anyone challenging the true depth of my trust. As far as I was concerned Jesus was not only the Son of God and the Saviour of Man, He was also my one true friend.

In my Actual Death Experiences, Jesus took me on a one to one journey with Him. He spoke of this journey as being 'the *Who Am I?* Journey of my Spirit'. It is a journey that everyone goes on after they have passed over into the afterlife, and the purpose of the journey is to teach us all the truth of our love. Not just our love for Him but in regard to everyone who we claim to have love for, including the love we have for ourselves. In one particular ADE Jesus showed me how little I truly understood the meaning of trust.

## Actual Death Experience
**Around The Earth In Its Global Form**

In the Spirit I became and Lord Jesus carried my Spirit away to become of His Teaching. He held my Spirit - keeping me safe within His protective embrace. We journeyed together into the heavens. I felt the wind beneath me, and folding around me like a blanket. The whispering breeze caught me - lifting me up higher and higher.

We soared into the voiceless echo's of the uncharted realms of His mystifying universe. Then Jesus held me suspended in the folds of Space. I became as a lantern without a rod, as He turned me slowly around to view my wondrous surroundings. In the distance, the stars twinkled brightly - then glowed softly, as if they were in a harmony together, exchanging a mysterious song.

Far below I caught sight of a global planet, and I knew in my senses that it was the planet earth.

In a moments rush, Jesus took my hand, and together we flew at a tremendous speed down towards the planet earth. Then we journeyed around the planet in its global form, and we returned back into the universe. Once again I was caught suspended in Space. Jesus then returned my Spirit back into my Physical body, and I became of my physical life again.

In an Actual Death Experience that followed this incredible ADE, Jesus explained His teaching to me,

*"I have carried your Spirit around the Earth in its global form and returned your Spirit safely back into your body - why do you still not trust?"*

His revelation came as a shock to me. How could Jesus say I didn't trust Him? I was mortified. I loved Jesus with all my heart and trusted Him completely. It would be ludicrous not to trust Him. Sadly, what we think we believe and what we truly believe are often very different.

If I truly trusted Jesus then why was I so afraid of my Actual Death Experiences. I'd been having ADEs for years, yet still, every night, I would lie on my bed clutching hold of my crucifix, praying to Jesus not to come and take me in an ADE. How could a reality of meeting with Jesus be so beautiful, and yet also so very frightening at the same time?

In truth, it was my fear that created my lack of trust. I knew I was protected and safe with Jesus but subconsciously I could not come to terms with the fact that I was experiencing the physical death. I was terrified by my reality. I was a wife and a young mother, and I loved my life. I loved being a mother. I desperately wanted to be a good mother - to share in all the irreplaceable moments that having children brings. Their unconditional love was truly sacred. The beauty of their innocence and trust took my breath away. They needed me to protect them, to always keep them safe, to ensure they were kept warm and never went hungry, to teach them about life. They depended on me with their lives, and I just couldn't bear the thought of ever having to leave them.

Over and over again, Jesus proved he would always bring me back from the physical death, and I would live to see my children again. But no matter how hard I tried, I could not let the fear of death leave my thoughts. The fear was always there with me throughout their childhood, casting its shadow over my life.

Jesus asks us to follow Him, and if we do He promises to lead us away from temptation. He will guide us to the New Earth, where we can live with Him in paradise. The scriptures are very clear in this understanding; especially in Jesus, the Light of the World (John 8: 12) Jesus said to the people,

*"I am the light of the world. If you follow me, you won't be stumbling through the darkness, because you will have the light that leads to life".*

When Jesus teaches us the truth of our love, it is not just about how true our trust in Him truly is but He also teaches us the truth for why our Spiritual bodies have developed certain characteristic traits, and how these often unnoticed flaws to us hinder our Spiritual growth.

In my love for Jesus, I never doubted for a single moment my desire to follow Him, then within another ADE, He showed me a truth within my acceptance to follow Him that I didn't know existed.

## Actual Death Experience
### The Marble Steps

In the Spirit I became and Lord Jesus carried my Spirit away to become of His Teaching. He held my Spirit in His loving embrace - protecting me from all harm. In the distance I saw a shaded tunnel and there at the end of the tunnel I could see a small circle of light. We journeyed together through the tunnel towards the bright light. As we neared the light - the light became brighter, turning upon itself, as if it was a giant ball spinning around.

In the air all around, I sensed an electrifying spark of energy - then moments later the bright blinding light engulfed my entire senses as we became caught-up within His majestic throne. I drifted along; being carried by His love - moving slowly through a sky of soft white clouds with sparkling silver threads glittering their edges.

I began to feel myself slowly descend, and suddenly I found myself standing upon the New Earth. There I saw I was standing with a group of other people, all of whom I knew instantly belonged to this Earth. We were all stood two by two in a line. I was standing at the back of the line next to a person, I had never met before. We began to walk slowly forwards, and I noticed Jesus was ahead of us leading the group.

Then the most incredible marble steps appeared in front of us, animating my entire surroundings, and Jesus began to lead us up the marble steps. The marble shimmered with a gold inlay - patterning the outline of leaves with diamond encrusted stems.

Suddenly, I became overwhelmed with a desire to walk with Jesus. I didn't like being at the end of the line and behind the others. I wanted to be walking next to Him. I stepped out of the line and quickly ran up past the others, climbing up the marble steps with a heightened eagerness as I got closer to Lord Jesus. When I finally reached His side. I was elated, delighted that no one had tried to stop me from getting my own way in what I had wanted.

At that moment Jesus told me to look down at my feet, and when I did, I saw that my left foot was very slightly in front of His right foot. Then I saw the marble step underneath my foot disappear. I was convinced I was going to fall forwards, and panic swept through my entire being.

Jesus then brought His left foot forward, and as He did the marble step re-appeared underneath His foot. I knew to step away and return back to my place at the end of the line. Jesus then returned my Spirit back into my Physical body, and I became of my physical life again.

## Are You My Lord Jesus?

In an Actual Death Experience that followed this incredible ADE, Jesus explained His teaching to me,

*"Do not walk beside me or in front of me but follow me. I will protect you and always keep you safe... The conceited child burdens his Spirit with a mighty cross. Be remaining humble for blessed are the meek for they will inherit the earth".*

I can remember being emotionally overwhelmed by Jesus' teaching for want of my 'egotism' in the fact that I felt I had a 'right' to walk beside Jesus. I didn't and I don't. Jesus didn't die upon the cross, so we can walk beside Him. He sacrificed His life, so we could walk with Him by following Him. He is the light and so He will lead us.

I once met a female minister who by all accounts, and for good reason she was a very popular preacher but ten minutes after our conversation started - her words had me physically cringing. After telling her I had chronic Actual Death Experiences, and I am meeting with Jesus in the Spiritual experiences - she made the bold claim,

*"I have met Jesus as well".*

I was curious and I very politely asked her to tell me about it. *"One day I heard a knock at my front door, and when I answered it was Jesus standing there".* She continued on with her explanation. *"I lead Him into my lounge to where my husband was sitting. I said to my husband, 'you know who this is don't you? Then I introduced Jesus to my husband".*

I realised as soon as she said 'she opened her door and saw Jesus standing there' that she didn't mean Jesus was physically standing at her front door' but her choice of words - her belief was that she lead Jesus into her lounge and her husband had never met Him before - hence the need of her introduction.

In the next chapter - *The Relationship of Consciousness between the Physical Mind and the Spiritual Mind* - you'll read about 'the power of thought' and how our thoughts govern our Spiritual growth. It is essentially important that we don't place ourselves by means of our thoughts in a position where our Spirit's come to believe that we would ever walk in front of Jesus. No matter how innocently we might be in the telling of a story. If we believe in the story in our love for Him - then our Spirits will believe it is how we see Him in our love for Him.

Showing me within the ADE that my foot went just slightly in front of His, and as a result the marble step suddenly disappeared was indeed a beautiful way to teach me that I had not fully understood His sacrifice and in thus my relationship with Him. It was the perfect way to teach the Child within me to behave with more respect and take my rightful place in following Him.

## *Who Am I? -The Journey*

*No life is more important than another.
And nothing has been without purpose - nothing.*

*We are all part of a great pattern.
That we, someday, may understand.*

*And one-day when we alone, have done,
what we are capable of doing.*

*We get to rise-up and reunite with those
we have loved the most.*

*Forever Embraced.*

# 3

# The Relationship of Consciousness
## Between
# The Physical Mind and The Spiritual Mind

In an Actual-Death Experience; Jesus told me that I would come to understand I have a 'child within myself', and it was my responsibility to teach that child about love and to understand the truth of my teachings within my own physical life. In this realisation we are indeed each our own teacher in life.

I learned that the child within is my Spirit, and the reason for my Actual Death Experiences was for Jesus to teach me the truth of my own teachings, even unto my own Spirit. Most of us actually live our physical lives not realising that we have an ongoing relationship with our Spirit.

In His teachings, Jesus explained that the physical mind is the 'Parent Mind' and the mind of the child within is the 'Spiritual Mind'. Both have an existence of consciousness. In my Actual Death Experiences, Jesus spoke about there being three conscious levels in our human existence: 1] The Conscious - our everyday thoughts, awareness and the logic of rationalisations, 2] The Second Conscious (the Subconscious), the level of protection, absorbing the 'thoughts/images' we do not require during the precise moment in time of conscious intake, and 3] The Consciousness of God (the Higher Consciousness).

The Second Conscious acts as a bridge connecting the Human Conscious with the Consciousness of God. The understanding that we are all 'children of God' lies in the Consciousness of God being of the Spiritual Mind, the mind of your own Spirit - the child within you. And whereas the physical mind requires 'thoughts of knowledge' to develop and mature constructively, the Spiritual mind needs to have 'thoughts of love' to grow an abundance of positive energy. In this sense the human Spirit is the 'core' of all man's emotions. The child within is the key to understanding our 'hearts', and just as we have a physical brain, so we also have a Spiritual brain. The Spiritual brain is the conscience aspect of our consciousness.

In life we become involved in many different relationships. The most influential relationships of them all are those that teach us about love. These relationships have three simple needs that must be given and received by the parties involved for the relationship to develop and grow into a strong, wellbalanced, healthy and positive one. These three essential needs are: 1] *Trust*, 2] *Respect*, and 3] *Security*.

If you do not *trust* your partner, you will never feel you are able to believe in the relationship. If you do not have *respect* for your partner, you will never put any value in the relationship. If you do not feel *secure* with your partner, you will never feel safe in the relationship.

We give our partners these three needs by our words and actions. When it comes to the relationship between the physical mind and the Spiritual mind, we have to give and receive the same three basic needs. The physical mind gives these needs to the Spiritual mind by having the thoughts: 1] *I trust myself,* 2] *I respect myself,* 3] *I feel secure in myself.* The Spiritual mind will return the needs of the physical mind within the emotions. When we are able to feel the emotion, we will acknowledge the feeling by having more positive thoughts about ourselves: I feel happy; I am proud of myself; I was right to make that decision, etc. The continuing positive thoughts are regenerating the positive emotions which we can then physically feel.

## How Do I Teach My Spirit About Love?

Within life we use our physical mind to generate and harness our conscious thoughts, rationalising everything we do, say and believe in. We can be good. We can be bad. We can choose to believe in God. We can be guided by the rules of Atheism.

The first realisation to acknowledge is that within our physical lives we are each our own teacher. In this reality, our physical mind takes on the role of parent/teacher. The Spiritual mind is of the role child/student. We all have outside influences in the building of our character, but it is our *free will* that also denotes how we come to perceive life, as the *thought process* that creates who we are in our status of existence.

In having the gift of free will, we ultimately have

## The Relationship of Consciousness

total control over our own physical lives. We can either live our lives in peace - free from emotional suppression, or live life with a constant feeling of sadness burdened with self-doubt and feelings of unworthiness. If for whatever reason you find yourself without the ability to use your free will to make the positive changes that you want within your life because of your outside influences, then firstly you must remove yourself from the restriction. For example: If you find yourself suffering from an abusive marriage, you need *time out* away from the relationship, so you can assess things freely in your own time and without the outside influence; reflect upon how you feel about the relationship and what you need to do to make the positive changes you are wanting to. You can decide either to end the marriage or to continue with the relationship. Whatever you do decide, it has to be on your own terms, because it is your own feelings of unhappiness that you are trying to understand and work through.

The main point to realise is that it is the thoughts from our physical mind that act as *instructions* to our Spiritual mind, which is why the physical mind has the role of parent/teacher. Unlike within our physical life, where we are usually judged by the actions we perform and the *words* we speak to others, the Spiritual mind only listens and learns from our thoughts. If our thoughts are not the same as the words we speak, and opposed to our actions - then we are without realisation *forcing our Spirit into conflict* with the instructions of the teacher - our physical mind. In the relationship of the consciousness, our Spirit is learning every day from what we call *the transcript of our life.*

Every good thought, every bad thought is instructing our Spiritual growth from the moment we are mature enough to understand and use our own free will. You wouldn't stand in front of a classroom of children as their teacher, and then promptly teach them the opposite to everything written within the text book you have provided for the lesson; so why verbally say the opposite to what you are actually thinking? We teach our Spirit by having the positive thoughts of love, both towards ourselves and towards others. But to ensure our Spirit does not reject our instructions, we must also speak the same words as our thoughts, and our actions should then result from this balance.

### *Understanding the Cycle*

The physical mind produces the thought. The spiritual mind creates the emotion within the Spirit. The emotion is transmitted by means of a *heat source* to the Spiritual brain. The Spiritual brain sends a signal via the Spiritual mind to the physical brain to trigger a physical reaction.

## The Relationship of Consciousness

```
                    ┌─────────────────────┐
                    │  The Physical Brain │
                    └─────────────────────┘
┌──────────────────┐                          ┌──────────────────┐
│ The Third-Conscious│                        │  The Conscious   │
└──────────────────┘                          └──────────────────┘
┌──────────────────┐                          ┌──────────────────┐
│ The Spiritual Mind│                         │ The Physical Mind│
└──────────────────┘                          └──────────────────┘

┌──────────────────┐                          ┌──────────────────┐
│ The Spiritual Mind│                         │ The Physical Mind│
└──────────────────┘                          └──────────────────┘

┌────────┐  ┌──────────────┐  ┌────────────────┐  ┌────────┐
│ Shared │←─│ The Conscience│←─│ The Sub-Conscious│  │ Shared │
└────────┘  └──────────────┘  └────────────────┘  └────────┘
                    ┌─────────────────────┐
                    │  The Spiritual Brain│
                    └─────────────────────┘
```

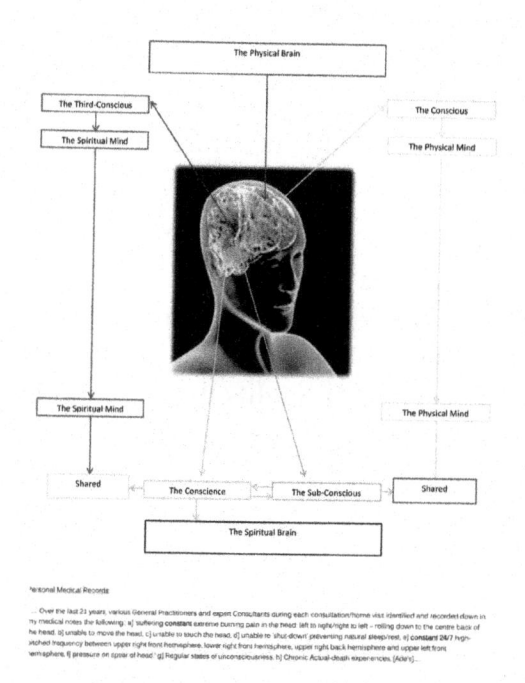

*Personal Medical Records*

*... Over the last 21 years, various General Practitioners and expert Consultants during each consultation/home visit identified and recorded down in my medical notes the following; a] suffering **constant** extreme burning pain in the head: left to right/right to left - rolling down to the centre back of the head, b] unable to move the head, c] unable to touch the head, d] unable to shut down/ preventing natural sleep/rest, e] **constant 24/7** high-pitched frequency between upper right front hemisphere, lower right front hemisphere, upper right back hemisphere and upper left front hemisphere, f] pressure on (rear of head.' g] Regular states of unconsciousness. h] Chronic Actual-death experiences. [ADE's]...*

*Above - Diagram: Outlining the trace of the heat source between the physical mind and the Spiritual mind, and between the physical brain and the Spiritual brain. This heat-source trace has only been made possible under medical supervision for my chronic Actual-Death Experiences*

## The Physical Brain and the Spiritual Brain

When we are sad (an emotion), we produce tears (a physical reaction). When we are happy (an emotion), we produce the sound of laughter (a physical reaction). If we did not have a Spiritual brain, we would not know how to react o our many different emotions.

The Spiritual brain is to the Spiritual body as the physical brain is to the physical body. For example, if you accidentally touch a hot stove, the nerves in your skin shoot a message of pain to your brain. The brain then sends a message back telling the muscles in your hand to pull away. The same principle occurs when you have taught yourself to have sad thoughts in association with a reality or memory within your physical life. When you have such a sad thought within your physical mind, the emotion is acknowledged by your Spiritual mind and the emotion is produced in your Spirit. The Spirit then sends a message to the Spiritual brain for the understanding of the actual emotion produced, which then triggers the Spiritual mind to associate the emotion with the reality or memory (the original thought process, i.e. the original thought of sadness). The Spiritual mind then sends a signal to the physical brain to prompt a physical reaction: the neurons in the limbic system are triggered to produce the tears.

The make-up of the Spiritual Brain is the *conscience* aspect of the consciousness. The more we are taught and teach ourselves about morality - the value of life, the difference between right and wrong, having a greater awareness for other people's needs, taking responsibility for ourselves, our own actions, society and the human

## The Relationship of Consciousness

race - then the more developed our Spiritual brain becomes.

In understanding the reality of having a physical and a spiritual mind (*the mind of your spirit*), and realising that our thought process acts as a source of communication between the two, we can establish an ready relationship between our physical and our spiritual existence; and the three principal needs of this relationship are the same ones that govern all our other relationships in life. The relationship between the physical mind and the spiritual mind has one fundamental purpose: to develop and maintain a state of equilibrium in life. Both must give and receive from the other the three primary needs: 1] *Trust,* 2] *Respect,* and 3] *Security.* Our physical mind conveys these needs to our spiritual mind by means of our thoughts. Our spiritual mind conveys these needs to our physical mind by means of our emotions.

### *How to Achieve a State of Equilibrium in Life*

The power behind the thought is in believing the thought to be true. First acknowledge you are having a positive thought about yourself, and accept it is good to have such positive thoughts. It is pointless to have a positive thought such as *I trust myself,* and then allow a negative one to follow straight after: But do I truly trust myself? How can I trust myself? If we allow a negative thought to follow a positive thought, we are teaching our Spirit to doubt our own teachings, resulting in mixed emotions being created - the feelings of good one minute, then doubt the next.

We are literally confusing our own Spirit, which is denying our Spiritual mind of its three basic needs, trust, respect and security, which will produce feelings of distrust, disrespect and insecurity. When these emotions are picked up by our physical mind, they will simply generate more negative thoughts. The cycle becomes very destructive within our life. Once we have accepted that we do have the ability, which is good, to trust ourselves, to respect ourselves and to feel secure in the decisions we make about our life, then our Spirit will respond to such a thought with the emotion associated with it: the feeling of positivity.

### The Empty Emotional Feeling in Life

The empty emotional feelings in life are created when the thoughts of the physical mind are not being acted upon by the individual creating the thoughts. This causes the individual's Spirit to *reject* his or her own teachings, and the Spirit does not respond with an emotion.

### Understanding the Feeling of Emptiness

For example, in a once loving physical relationship between a man and a woman, the man is now no longer having thoughts of love (I love her) for the woman. He becomes consumed with such thoughts as, 'I don't love her any more. I am not happy in this relationship. I don't want to be with her any more...' etc. However, the man does not end the relationship, and he continues to speak words of love to the woman, ('Of course I love you!).

In the majority of these cases, the reason the man

gives himself for not ending the relationship is that he still feels an attachment towards the woman, and does not want to hurt her, which he believes he will do if he ends the relationship. He is unaware that his sense of attachment is being generated by his thoughts of how good the relationship once was - his *memories,* rather than the actual current reality of his relationship with the woman.

In continuing to have the thoughts that he no longer wants to be in a relationship with the woman, while yet remaining with her, he is not acting upon the *truth* of his thoughts, his own teachings of love. He is now denying himself one of the basic needs of his Spiritual mind - *respect* for his own love. He will eventually come to start thinking and treating the woman with disrespect. If his Spiritual brain – his conscience – is healthily developed, he will come to acknowledge within his thoughts that how he is thinking and acting towards the woman is wrong, and he will generate feelings of mistrust for his own teaching of love within his Spirit. He is now denying himself another basic need of his Spiritual mind: *trust* for his own love.

If the man continues to deny himself (*his Spirit*) the truth of his thoughts in his actions, his Spiritual mind will begin to reject all of his own 'instructions', his *thoughts of love,* and he will soon be unable physically to feel any emotion of love within his heart. The man will only be able to sense a feeling of *emptiness* within his heart whenever he thinks of love, and he will thus be denying himself the third basic need of the Spiritual mind: *security.* He will no longer feel secure within his own teachings of love, which will eventually have him doubting love or the belief that he is worthy of love, and such feelings will hinder the possibility of his falling in love again, as his actions contradict the truth of his thoughts.

In continuing with the relationship, he is doing something he doesn't truly want to do. His Spiritual mind will emit uncertainty and confusion about the emotions of love. His physical mind will pick up on a sense of disorder in acknowledging that his physical actions countermand the truth of his thoughts. This will then cause the man to question his full understanding of his own love, producing further thoughts of doubt such as, Why am I still with her when I do not love her any more?

If the Physical mind (*the decision maker - the aspect of rationalisation*) refuses to listen to the Spiritual mind and does not act upon the thought, a state of emotional crisis is created: I have no *trust* in relationships. I do not believe in love. I am *insecure* in love. Essentially, by his own free will, he has created his own feeling of emptiness within his heart.

In understanding the needs of our Spirit now, while we are still in the physical life, we are taking control of both the physical and the Spiritual aspects of our life. In understanding the human consciousness and our Spiritual origin, we can learn how to improve our own lives. The new-found knowledge can free us from all forms of unhealthy social and religious domination.

We do not have to live in a darkness created by our joint misconceptions of life. We have the ability to repair and rebuild our broken societies. We have the ability to put war and world destruction behind us. We have the ability to live in peace as mankind evolves into a Higher Consciousness for life.  Our Spirit is tapped into the Spiritual energy within the universe. God is the creator of that same positive energy: His Unconditional Love.

## The Teachings of Jesus
### Within an Actual-Death Experience

*As I sat with Jesus upon the New Earth, He said
unto my Spirit, "If you do not know me.
How will you recognise me when I come?
If you do not know yourself - as the child of God.
How will you ever know me?
And this is of God's spoken promise to
His children still waiting to follow me into paradise,
If you do not know the child of God
You will not know the Son of God.
And if you do not know the Son of God
You will not know the Father."*

# 4

## The Controversial Enlightenment

The kindly old Priest shook his head as he walked in step with me through the picturesque gardens of the Church. In his fingers he held an unlit half-smoked cigarette, and his worn black robes aired layers of a strong tobacco odour. While his nose and high cheeks were reddened by the consumption of vast quantities of alcohol, his facial features bore the look of a man who had seen many things in life; engraving harsh haunting memories, if the glint of sadness reflecting in his eyes was a true insight into this man's soul.

He seemed troubled by my words, as if they had fallen upon his ears in a riddle.

"*I don't understand,*" he said finally. "*What has Jesus got to do with the Fairy Tale?*"

I took a deep breath and sighed wearily for his questioning tone. My companion was lost within the world of opinion instigated by man's translations of the holy scriptures. *Why did he not hear the beating heart of Jesus in my words?* A revelation of pure untainted love - so precious, it belonged only to the beauty of innocence.

I felt an overwhelming desire to continue my

conversation. I wanted him to understand my love, so he too could join in the celebrations for the teachings of Jesus. But then I suddenly remembered the words Jesus had spoken in one of my Actual Death experiences: *"Do not try to teach those who do not wish to be taught; for your words will fall upon deaf ears and frustration will become of your heart."*

## Actual Death Experience
### Before Him - We Shall Sit

As I fell into the first folds of physical death, Jesus stood by my bedside waiting. He commanded my Spirit to rise up out of my physical body, and as I passed over into the Afterlife, He carried my Spirit away, holding me safely in His warm, tender embrace.

We journeyed together, flashing through His infinite universe like an electrifying bolt of lightning. I felt the sweeping wind brush against my face as I touched destiny within the silent moods of the great mystery beyond the shadows.

We passed the stars illuminating His miracle. Storms of emotions took me, raging with fury, and lifted my love up into the thunderous skies of His heavens, shooting my heart towards a bright dazzling tunnel of light. I felt safe, engulfed in the radiance of His majestic crown. My whole being was caught up within the glowing passageway of life.

When His flight was over, I became of the New Earth, and a blanket of peace folded around me, as if I were still held in the arms of Christ. I suddenly felt content, and even in my bewilderment at the purpose of

## The Controversial Enlightenment

my journey with Him, I felt no urge to question His will.

I looked around at my surroundings, and noticed I was sitting on the ground in the middle of a large group of people who all belonged to this earth. The ground beneath me was softened by a layer of sand, and the vast landscape glowed with a warm, golden yellow colour; a terrain where small clusters of huge rocks rooted between thick, lush green rounded bushes and olive trees.

Then I saw Jesus sitting down upon a large rocky boulder in front of us, and I knew we were all waiting to hear Him speak. In the far distance behind Him I saw three hills, and at the very top of each one I saw erected a large wooden cross. At that moment I realised I had been brought here to witness the New Jerusalem. Then I heard Jesus begin to speak:

*"Why follow the light of another, when in your own hand you hold the brightest light of all - the light of your own love. Do not carry the cripple who can walk, or lead the blind man with sight. Do not try to teach those who do not wish to be taught; for your words will fall upon deaf ears and frustration will become of your heart. If your heart knows only frustration, then you too will become blind to the kingdom of God."*

Jesus continued to teach us about God's love, and when He had finished, I felt myself being caught up in His love again as He returned my Spirit back into my physical body, and breathed life back into me once again.

In remembering the teachings of Jesus, I knew it would be wrong for me to continue in my conversation with the Priest. The Priest had his own beliefs, which I had to respect if I was to deliver Jesus' *Who Am I?* prophecies in their true understanding: *"Why follow the light of another, when in your own hand you hold the brightest light of all - the light of your own love."*

Jesus' message is primarily about learning to understand yourself - your own love. Why do you love as you do? Why do you love the people whom you have chosen to love? Are you true to your love by conviction and in your thoughts? - meaning, *Do your convictions in life honour your love, or do you say and do things that are against your love?*

We all have choices in life and our own free will usually determines the choices we make. But before we can decide if we are being true to ourselves we must first understand our love - not just in how and why we love others, but also in how we love ourselves.

After my encounter with the elderly Priest, I thanked him for his time and left his company, but as I walked away I felt a brief sense of sadness for his *vocal expectation* in his love for Jesus. He believed that if I was truly with Jesus in the Spirit, then I would be able to recite the scriptures to memory. I would come from a background of a strict religious education, and I would belong to a Church in constant daily attendance.

When I explained to him that I didn't belong to any one Church, and I had never had a religious upbringing, my two admissions of truth had not rested easily with the Priest. So it was no surprise that when I also revealed that Jesus had given me the teachings of a Fairy Tale within my Actual Death Experiences, and that in several He had taken my Spirit to meet with the Spirit of the late Walt Disney, the Priest could not comprehend the truth of my own love, and he struggled to accept I was with Christ in the Spirit as His witness.

The sadness I'd felt as I had walked away wasn't because the Priest had not believed my testimonial. It was for the expectation that governed his love for Jesus. In his belief and expectation of those before whom Jesus would appear, making them His witness, the Priest was forgetting it is Jesus who decides such; not man. Everything is done according to His will, and all Jesus asks of us is to be prepared and ready to follow Him.

In deciding who Jesus would and would not make His witness, the Priest was not allowing Jesus to lead him. Instead, he himself was laying down the path of Our Lord's steps. If I had asked the Priest, "Do you believe Jesus would love a woman who came from a broken home and didn't go to Church in the same way as he would love a woman from a loving family home who attends Church every week?" I know the Priest would have replied, "Yes of course he does"

If I had then asked, "Do you also believe Jesus would appear before a woman he loves?" his answer would have naturally been, "Yes of course he would." So why then did the Priest have doubts over my testimonial when I am a woman who comes from a broken home, a woman who did not have a strong religious background and a woman who did not attend Church? If I had simply changed the composition of my conversation with the Priest, he would have answered me with a truth he believed that was opposite to his belief of me.

This is a very important aspect of understanding the *essence of our own love*, the love we have taught our own Spirit within our physical lives. It is about being true to ourselves - our thoughts, and respecting the *teacher* that is within us all. It is about following the light of our own sweet love. The light we hold within our own hand.

### The Physical Body and the Spiritual Body

The physical body is the flesh, the outer shell - 'the temple.' The scriptures refer to it as such: *Do you not know that your bodies are temples of the Holy Spirit, who is in you, whom you have received?* (Corinthians 6:19).

In my Actual Death Experiences, Jesus taught me that we also have a Spiritual body, and when we pass over into the Afterlife from the physical death, we pass over within our Spiritual body. I was permitted to witness that the appearance of our Spiritual body is of the same image as our physical body at the time of physical death. The only difference I saw was when the physical body had been maimed by a birth, medical or accidental disfigurement, as the Spiritual body does not have any disabilities.

I was then shown that our Spiritual body goes through a series of changes in appearances. These changes reveal the truth of the teachings we have taught ourselves within our physical life. If we have lived our physical life being consumed with bad thoughts and committing evil deeds, then our Spiritual Body will

## The Controversial Enlightenment

reflect the truth of our teachings with an ugliness, (*see ADE: The Dancing Demons of the Evil Mind*). However, if we have lived our physical life nurturing good thoughts, positivity and kindness etc., then our Spiritual Body will reflect our beauty.

Following the transition through changes of appearance, we then go through a period of learning. Jesus spoke of this learning period as being The *Who Am I?* journey of our Spirit. This is not a time of judgement, but rather a journey of knowledge in a time of reflection: a time to reflect upon everything we had taught ourselves in our role as *Teacher* within our physical life.

In the *Who Am I?* journey of our Spirit, Jesus now becomes our Teacher. In the physical death, we leave behind the physical mind, thus leaving behind our Teacher within. In our new Spiritual existence we are no longer able to use logical thought in teaching ourselves the reason for our actions.

For Example: if you smoked during your physical life, then you will still be a smoker within your Spiritual body - your Spiritual existence. But unlike within your physical life, when you were your own *teacher* and had the ability to teach yourself it was wrong to smoke, you now no longer have this ability. Now Jesus comes as your Teacher and teaches you it is wrong. He walks with you throughout the *Who Am I?* journey of your Spirit, and through him you learn to understand the truth of your own teachings within the physical mind. He guides the child in you to understand whether you were right or wrong, giving you the truth of the consequences for your thoughts and actions. He leads you to an *acceptance stage* for the belief you held for your paradise; showing you how your thoughts and actions within your physical life contradicted your other beliefs.

For example, the individual who is a smoker within their physical life, who also accepts that heaven is paradise with God, would not realise that you cannot enter the Kingdom of God if you are a smoker. It is the same with swearing (*see ADE The Swear Word Is Muted In Heaven*) and alcohol abuse (*see ADE Learn To Do As You Are Told, Beverley*). I had always been a frequent smoker, and although I knew it was very unhealthy to smoke, I had no reason to believe my smoking habit was causing me any other harm. But then Jesus showed me exactly what I was doing to my Spiritual body in having a tobacco addiction.

## Actual Death Experience
### Is This Your Paradise?

I became of the Spirit within the Afterlife. There I found myself standing before Christ in a place that was not of this earth (the old earth), nor was it a place of the New Earth. I knew only that I was standing within the clouds in a place of reflection and knowledge.

In the distance and to the left hand side of Jesus, I suddenly saw a huge, dark, murky lake of tar. It was a sight I did not find pleasing to the eye and I wondered why Jesus was showing me such. Then I noticed several people moving around within the lake. They were trying to stand up and walk out of the lake. Only their Spiritual bodies were covered in the black murky tar, and each time they attempted to stand up, the black tar covering them weighed them down, pulling them back into the lake. I stood watching in terror as I witnessed their torment, and all I could hear within the heavens were the screams of their extreme agony.

I looked across at Jesus, who was standing tall with His arms by His sides. In that instant, He began to raise His arms into the air, and as they rose up sideways, clouds of smoke suddenly appeared surrounding my Spiritual body. The smoke was thick, like a dense fog, blocking everything from my sight. Now I was no longer able to see the lake of tar and I couldn't even see Jesus standing in front of me, but I knew He was still there for I heard Him ask of me, "Is this your Paradise?"

He then returned my Spirit back into my physical body and breathed life into me once again.

Jesus had been teaching me about what my smoking addiction was doing to my Spiritual body. I just hadn't realised that something as simple as smoking had such a negative impact on our eternal life. Instantly I wanted to give up smoking, and I tried many times unsuccessfully. Every time I put a cigarette into my mouth and lit it, I felt dreadful. I knew I was giving into temptation.

I scolded myself for being so weak, and I felt unworthy of His teachings. *Why couldn't I just show Him how much I truly loved Him and stop smoking? Why was it so difficult?* On reflection, it was probably the main conflict I've always had during my journey with Him. I wanted to show Him that I was strong, my love for Him untainted. Time and time again I would give up smoking, only to start again later. Then I'd give up once more.

I had to face the harsh reality of my truth: in truth, I didn't want to give up smoking. I enjoyed having a cigarette too much, especially with my morning coffee. I was constantly making excuses for why I was still smoking, and forever apologising to Jesus through normal prayer; asking Him to forgive me for my weakness.

Regardless of how many excuses I made, I could not escape the truth of my own teachings within my physical life. I smoked because I wanted to, and every time I had a cigarette, I was creating a smoke-filled paradise of misery in a murky lake of tar for my Spiritual body. The only way I could change this horrendous future I was creating was to give up smoking for good.

I knew it would never happen until I changed the way I was thinking, within my thought process. Instead of thinking, *I'll just have one more cigarette, it won't do any harm,* or, *I just need a cigarette to calm my nerves,* I had to start instructing myself to have the thoughts, I don't need a cigarette - smoking is bad for my health. How can I live with Jesus upon the New Earth if I am creating a paradise of smoke?

In life we must learn to take responsibility for our own actions, those governed by our own free will. The most important thing to understand is that you are your own teacher within your physical life, so everything has to start from you - your thoughts, your actions. The same applies if you are a heavy drinker. Instead of thinking, *I like drinking, I enjoy having a drink,* start changing your thoughts to, *I don't like drinking, I don't need to drink.* It's *not good for me.* In understanding the relationship of consciousness, every time you have the thoughts I need a drink, I have to have a drink, I won't feel better until I've had a drink, I'd love to have a drink right now, you are essentially associating the *want* of alcohol with an *emotion of love.* Your need for alcohol has become based on what you are teaching yourself is an instruction of love, I'd love a drink right now. Your Spiritual mind will respond to the thought of I want a drink with the feelings of love from your Spirit. This emotional attachment then causes you to have that yearning desire within you to drink alcohol, which will not fade until after you have had the drink. Therefore, through your own teachings - the thoughts of your physical mind, you are creating the addiction within your life.

## After Death Experience
### Learn To Do As You Are Told Beverley

I became of the Spirit within the Afterlife. There I found myself standing before Christ in a place that was not of this earth, the old earth, nor was it a place of the New Earth. I knew only that I was standing within the clouds in a place of reflection and knowledge.

In the distance I saw the figure of a man walking towards me. As he came closer, I realised it was the Spirit of my late father John Gilmour, who had passed over in 1982. It was the first time Jesus had taken my Spirit to meet with my dad's Spirit. His appearance was the same as when he had passed over, aged fifty-two. A sudden surge of love filled my entire senses. I loved my dad dearly and I missed him. Now his presence before me overwhelmed me. I wanted to hug him and ask him so many questions, but I couldn't as I was not allowed to speak. I knew only, I was there to listen.

Suddenly I heard my dad say the words, *Learn to do as you are told, Beverley*. Then he just stood there without saying another word. I was confused. What did he mean, I had to learn to do as I was told? Why hadn't he told me how happy he was to see me and how much he loved me? Why hadn't he told me not to worry about him? Did he not know that I thought about him every day?

As I stood looking at him, I sensed he was staring straight at me, but at the same time I could see that our eyes were not meeting. His gaze seemed to be focused to my left. I also noticed that he seemed to be enframed in something apparently three-dimensional. Jesus then returned my Spirit back into my physical body and breathed life into me once again.

I wrote earlier in the Who Am I? prophecies of Jesus, 1993-1996, that this particular Actual Death Experience reveals several Spiritual teachings. The first concerns what becomes of our Spirit if we abuse alcohol within our physical lives. In his physical life, my dad had been a very heavy drinker. He would start drinking alcohol as soon as he woke up in the morning and continue drinking throughout the day. He eventually died on October 9th 1982 from cirrhosis of the liver.

In this ADE, Jesus was teaching me the reality of the Who Am I? journey of my dad's Spirit created by his alcohol abuse. The three-dimensional surrounding of his Spirit represented the familiar sense of the *physical displacement* that usually occurs after an individual has had too much alcohol. When my dad was staring straight at me, but our eyes were not meeting, he was actually having double vision, and so he was staring at his illusion of me.

The second aspect of this ADE is in the words my dad spoke to me, *Learn to do as you are told, Beverley.* I can remember that my initial thoughts after recovering from this particular ADE were of disappointment, which then provoked a sudden roller coaster ride of emotions. The sheer disappointment I first felt was in my dad's message. It was just so austere, not at all in character. We had always been very close and we had a very loving relationship. Even though he was constantly under the influence of alcohol, he was never an angry or violent man. He was always ready with a hug whenever I felt sad. On reflection, I can't remember there ever being a time when my dad actually disciplined me. We just didn't have that kind of relationship.

My parents were divorced when I was three years old, and I lived with my mother, so I would only get to see my dad once or twice a week. I remember him being a very good storyteller, and we would spend our time together telling each other jokes; he would often tease me with his dry sense of humour. In many senses, I was the typical spoilt little girl, as he would give me anything I asked for without a second thought.

I can remember on one occasion, I went to visit him with my high school sweetheart, Francis-John. Francis went into Woolworth's to buy a music record, and I went to meet my dad at the pub. I was thirteen years old and I was feeling utterly miserable because I didn't have any money to buy a record. After I finished complaining to my dad about how unfair it was, he suddenly disappeared and left me waiting outside the pub for Francis. Twenty minutes later he reappeared. He was waving an airline ticket up in the air and beaming a satisfied smile.

*"This should cheer you up, Pet. You are going to America to visit your sister for a holiday!"*

He had been at the travel agents and bought me the airline ticket to America. I was elated! I hugged him tightly and kissed him, as I jumped for joy. He was the best dad anyone could ever wish for.

This is how it always was with my dad, but I was too young to realise it wasn't really a healthy way to be raised. Our relationship was based on being friends rather than the normal parent-child relationship. My dad just didn't do the whole discipline routine.

Indeed, the ADE with my dad's Spirit had truly left me bewildered, and it wasn't until six years later, when I encountered my dad's Spirit for the second time within an ADE, that my dad was allowed to explain that he had been within the *Who Am I?* journey of his Spirit, in which Jesus had been teaching him the need and importance for a parent to discipline and have parental control over their children.

This was in 1992, and I was captivated by the difference in his appearance. He now looked much younger, healthier and stronger. His image reflected his life as he was within his late thirties. He spoke freely about love, and he was wise beyond comprehension. He did not need to tell me he was happy and at peace, his aura projected his love for me, and his feelings of contentment radiated around him. He was now of an eternal life with Jesus upon the New Earth. His Spiritual body now bore the image of a period in which he had been the most happy within his physical life.

Although the concept of time appears to have no reality within the Afterlife, the first two encounters I had with my dad's Spirit clearly indicate that the Who Am I? journey of our Spirit has a beginning and an end. In the Who Am I? prophecies of Jesus 1993-1996, it is written that the duration of the *Who Am I?* journey of our Spirit is different for everyone. In learning to understand our mistakes when Jesus becomes our teacher, and seeking his forgiveness, we are given the chance of changing our eternal future. Jesus also speaks of the resurrection as being of the Spiritual body, not the physical body (*see ADE The Great Golden Stairway*).

The greatest change I experienced after my first Actual Death Experience with my dad's Spirit was in my actual understanding of what was happening to me when I had an ADE, and this ultimate realisation took my emotions to the brink of despair. I was finally able to understand fully that I was experiencing the physical death and passing over into the Afterlife.

The sense of curiosity I'd first felt about the ADEs, which had allowed me to go through the motions, was now replaced by a deep-rooted fear - the fear of dying. The fear of not being able to make it back to see my daughter Samantha again. I wanted to be a mother. I wanted to see my little girl grow up and share with her all the precious moments that she would bring into my life: her first words, her first day at school, her first love, her wedding day, the birth of her children. I didn't want to be just a memory within her thoughts.

On reflection, I use to think if I had been able to control my Actual Death Experiences then I would not have been so afraid of them. I would have known I'd always be able to come back because I would always have chosen life over death. Samantha was just a baby, and even before she could utter her first word, her love was more than priceless to me. When I was beyond exhaustion and just wanted it all to end, simply to let go and not come back, I would feel Samantha in my heart. She was my love, and no matter how tired I felt or how sore my physical body became, I needed to be in her life. I needed to be her mother.

The unconditional love of a child has no boundaries. It can be felt in life as it can be felt within the Afterlife. A child's love is truly infinite.

## After Death Experience
### The Swear Word is Muted in Heaven

I became of the Spirit within the Afterlife. There I found myself standing before Christ in a place that was not of this earth, the old earth, nor was it a place of the New Earth. I knew only that I was standing within the clouds in a place of reflection and knowledge.

In the distance I saw the figure of a man waving his hand in my direction. The man began walking towards me and I knew he wanted to speak to me.

When he finally reached me, I looked at him closely, and although he was smiling at me as if he knew me, I did not recognise him. I sensed I had never actually met this man before and I became curious; wondering why he was there and why he wanted to speak to me.

Then without any vocal sounds being made, the man began speaking. But before he had even finished his first sentence, I noticed he wasn't making any sense, as there were several words missing from his sentence. I simply couldn't understand what he was saying. When he saw I was confused, he repeated his sentence, but again several words were missing. He sounded very strange and appeared to be speaking nonsense.

The man suddenly became frustrated. Sensing his annoyance, I did not want him to continue in conversation. The moment I told him I no longer wanted him to speak to me, he became silent. He was now unable to say another word whilst still in my company. Jesus then returned my Spirit back into my physical body and breathed life into me once again.

In the *Who Am I?* prophecies of Jesus 1993-1996, I wrote that this particular Actual Death Experience reveals how Jesus teaches us that the swear word, aka the curse word, is not accepted by God. If you are an individual who does think and frequently use swear words in your conversations, you are teaching your Spirit the same bad language, which is what happened to the Spirit of the man whom I encountered within this ADE. Jesus had muted his swear words, so this man's sentences did not make any sense and he was unable to converse with others. In some ways it is the same as smoking: would you really smoke a cigarette or a cigar in front of Jesus? Indeed you would not. So why do it when you know everything is revealed to Him when you pass over into the Afterlife. The question is the same: would you really use bad language in front of Jesus?

Within my ADEs, Jesus also came with the Fairy Tale, an enchanting magical story to remind me of the truth of how my love for Him first began within my childhood. Jesus teaches us the truth for every aspect of our love: the love we have for Him, the love we have for others, and the love we have for ourselves. I have always loved Jesus for as long as I can remember, but I had never placed any real importance on the origin of this love.

It began when I was a child, but the actual reason for this first love had become forgotten over the passing years of my physical life. When you pass over into the Afterlife and begin the Who Am I? journey of your Spirit with Jesus, imagine you are presenting Him with a garden - the garden of your life. Jesus then teaches you about the seeds that you have planted within your garden - giving you the raw truth of your love.

The reality I experienced within my childhood was of inconceivable conflict. On my father's side I had the Santa Claus family tradition. I would sit mesmerized, listening to my dad's stories of how when he was a young boy he grew up with his father, my Grandfather, being Santa Claus. Every Christmas Eve my Grandfather would be seen in his famous red suit pushing a hand cart down the cobble streets of Liverpool, and he would give out

## The Controversial Enlightenment

gifts to all the children who were excitedly awaiting his arrival. Then my dad would reveal with a twinkle in his eyes that the magic was still in our family with his brother, my Uncle Jim now being Santa Claus.

My Uncle Jim owned a Joke Shop in Wavertree, Liverpool, which he proficiently called The North Pole. It was decorated all year round in brightly coloured Christmas lights, white snow and sparkling tinsel, and the sounds of Christmas tunes were always playing softly in the background. There were toys everywhere, dolls, trains, and hundreds of both big and small Santas, Elves and Reindeer figurines.

I would clutch hold of my dad's hand in sheer excitement as we stepped into my Uncle Jim's magical grotto to be greeted by Santa Claus himself; hearing his jolly laugh and listening to his deep, velvet voice. Outside his shop, children were always gathered; their noses pressed up against the windows as they eagerly hoped to catch a glimpse of Santa Claus.

I knew he was my Uncle Jim, which just made it all even more special. I was the luckiest little girl in the world because I was related to Santa Claus, and I knew a secret that none of the other children knew. The North Pole Joke Shop wasn't just an ordinary joke shop; it was actually Santa's very own Secret Office, where all the children's letters went before they were collected by the Elves.

It was a childhood that knew of magic, laughter and love. But at the same time, my life was being scarred by the shadows of pain, caused by the immoral deeds of a child molester, a family member on my mother's side who had preyed upon me from when I was just a toddler scarcely able to walk, up until I was six years old. Then at that age I fell victim to a sexual assault by a stranger. I had been forced into a world of depravity and the wickedness of man's dark desires.

But then one day I encountered a King; a real King, and he lived in a big wondrous building so glorious and majestic, it was the perfect castle. I became His Princess alive in a beautiful never-ending Fairy Tale, in which my King came and rescued me from the fire-breathing dragon and then chased the darkness away.

Whenever I speak of how Jesus brought my Spirit the magical words of a Fairy Tale within my Actual Death Experiences, I am usually confronted with disbelief and rejection. It appears hard for people to understand what the teachings of Jesus have to do with a Fairy Tale. It is not the actual words of the Fairy Tale that is of any real importance. It is what the Fairy Tale represented within my childhood. It represented Love: the love I found for Jesus. He was my King and I was His little Princess. And now the childhood imagination I once had has created within my Actual Death Experiences a profound but most controversial Enlightenment...

## *The Fairy Tale*

### The Tree of the Gold Keys
### and the
### White Rose Princess

## *Autumn Rain*

*Do not stand at my grave and weep
I am not there. I do not sleep.
I am a thousand winds that blow.
I am the diamond glints on snow.
I am the sunlight on ripened grain.
I am the gentle autumn rain.*

*When you awaken in the morning's hush
I am the swift uplifting rush
Of quiet birds in circled flight.
I am the soft stars that shine at night.
Do not stand at my grave and cry;
I am not there. I did not die.*

*Mary Elizabeth Frye
[1932]*

# 5

# Forgiveness

*Forgiveness as with compassion
is one of the greatest gifts of a human being.*

**Matthew 6**

14: If you forgive those who sin against you, your heavenly Father will forgive you.

15: But if you refuse to forgive others, your Father will not forgive your sins.

What would you say if I told you that forgiveness is an important aspect of your Spiritual growth? I am sure you would answer, "It is obviously an important aspect,", or "Everyone knows it is important." True it is obviously important, and true everyone knows it is, but not everyone understands just how very significant it is to our Spiritual growth and why!

I once had a conversation with a man who told me he believed that even Hitler has a place in Heaven. If you believe he doesn't, then how do you make sense of the scriptures? We know Jesus is the Saviour of Man, and he died upon the Cross to save us from our sins - through Him our sins can be forgiven. But what we don't truly realise is that not everyone wants to be forgiven, and

## Forgiveness

some of us actually never reach forgiveness in our Spiritual growth. So what happens to those of us who *don't* seek forgiveness, or those who *can't* reach Spiritual forgiveness? Why can't they, and what becomes of them? Are they doomed for all eternity or is there a way back for them eventually to reach paradise with Jesus?

It is true, there is a place in Heaven for everyone, but paradise has to be earned, and you have to truly *want* it within your heart.

The scriptural verses of Matthew 6: 14-15 are a clear teaching from Jesus on forgiveness:

> *14: If you forgive those who sin against you, your heavenly Father will forgive you.*
>
> *15: But if you refuse to forgive others, your Father will not forgive your sins.*

In understanding the relationship of consciousness, and that we are each our own *Teacher* to the Child within, it is important that our *thoughts* are those of forgiveness for the people who have hurt us within our physical lives, just as it is equally important that we find the courage *truthfully* to seek forgiveness from anyone whom we may have hurt within our physical lives.

I understand this is easier said than done, but it is indeed the only way your Spirit will know forgiveness, and realise there may still be a need to seek forgiveness once you have passed over into the Afterlife and begun the *Who Am I?* journey of your Spirit with Jesus. If the Teacher in you does not teach yourself forgiveness within your physical life, you have a long journey ahead when you pass over into the Afterlife.

For example, within the *Who Am I?* journey of your Spirit, in showing you the truth of your love, Jesus may come to you and say,

*"What would you say if I told you - your wife/husband/friend has betrayed you?"*

Naturally you will respond with the same emotion that you would have experienced if you had discovered such a truth within your physical life - with the emotion of anger and feeling hurt for the betrayal. If the *Teacher* in you has taught yourself - *your thoughts* - to forgive others within your physical life, then you'll be able to reply to Jesus' question with, "*I forgive him/her for the betrayal*". Jesus will then take the emotion of anger away from your Spirit. In this way, He is *cleansing* your Spirit. He is taking away the pain that the act of betrayal has caused you, and your Spirit is becoming cleansed of the negative emotional energy – the emotion. Through His teachings your Spirit becomes of the unspoilt Spirit: the Child within, pure and blameless, free from all sin.

If your Spirit cannot reply, "*I forgive him/her for the betrayal*", Jesus will begin to teach you how to forgive, and He does this by showing you the truth of your love within the *Who Am I?* journey of your Spirit. He will show you a time when you had within your physical life betrayed another - every lie you have ever told.

For those of us who have a strong conscience, a healthy developed Spiritual brain, our response at being faced with our own act of betrayal is with the emotion of regret, which overwhelms our senses, and we will then ask Jesus to forgive us for the act of betrayal we have committed within our physical life.

We are now seeking forgiveness within the *Who Am I?* journey of our Spirit. Once we know how to seek forgiveness, our Spirit is able to understand the importance of being able to forgive others who have hurt us. Naturally, if the *Teacher* in us within our physical life has already taught us how to forgive, and to ask for forgiveness for our wrong-doings before we pass over into the Afterlife, then Jesus does not have to teach us such and our Spiritual growth happens much more rapidly.

This was a very interesting teaching to learn from Jesus, as many of us don't truly realise how understanding forgiveness affects the Spiritual body's growth.

Although it has to be remembered that there does not seem to be any concept of time within the Afterlife, the *physical* time-lapse between the first and the second time I met with my Dad's Spirit was five years. The first time I encountered his Spirit was in 1988, and his Spiritual body had the same appearance as when he passed over in 1982 at the age of fifty-two years. Then the second time I encountered his Spirit in 1992, his Spiritual body took on his appearance in his early thirties. It has to be stressed here that there is no 'night' within the Afterlife - the Spirit does not know of *sleep*, but from 1982 when he passed over, to 1992 when I met with him upon the New Earth totals ten years as the length of the *Who Am I?* journey of his Spirit with Jesus.

In 2006, I had an Actual Death Experience in which I encountered the Spirit of my late Grandmother. When I saw her, I witnessed her as still within the *Who Am I?* journey of her Spirit - even though she had entered the Afterlife in 1985, and her Spiritual body still had the appearance of when she first passed over Here we have a period of twenty-one physical years, indicating that her *Who Am I?* journey with Jesus has been longer than my dad's.

## After Death Experience
**I am Sorry About Your Mother**

I became of the Spirit within the Afterlife. There I found myself standing before Christ in a place that was not of this earth, the old earth, nor was it a place of the New Earth. I knew only that I was standing within the clouds in a place of reflection and knowledge.

My white surroundings appeared to be never ending; everywhere I looked, I sensed the softness of the mounting clouds moving slowly around.

Then in the distance I saw the figure of a woman approaching, and as she neared me I realised it was the Spirit of my Grandmother.

I knew not to speak for I sensed I was only there to receive a message, and I had to listen carefully as the message was very important to my Grandmother. Then I heard her say,

## Forgiveness

*"I am sorry about your Mother."*

Jesus then returned my Spirit back into my physical body and breathed life into me once again.

Although my Grandmother's message may at first appear to be of little importance, it is a major part of Spiritual growth, not just for my Grandmother but also for my own mother. In my Grandmother's physical life, her relationship with my mother was intense with negative emotions. There was a lot of bitterness, anger and spite, and the lack of maternal love from my Grandmother left my mother with little self-worth. With her confidence at a constant low, she always found herself making the wrong decisions, and it was the primary reason behind her unhealthy weight gain.

On hearing my Grandmother's apology for how she treated my mother, I felt it was important for me to discuss with my mother her feelings towards my Grandmother. I wanted her to let go of the sadness their relationship had caused her. It was very difficult. Her emotions of anger were buried so deep, she could not even *think* of her mother without feeling hurt and betrayed.

The Universe is made up of energy, both positive and negative. If you harbour grudges of resentment due to bad relationships, you are in essence fostering negative energy. In turn this will attract even more negative energy into your life. When you detect such energy around you, you will react with negative thoughts, which are unhealthy for your Spirit and affect your Spiritual growth within your physical life.

It is very difficult to truly forgive another person when they have brought pain into your life, especially if you have been a victim of crime but you have to find the courage to forgive him or her. If you don't, their negativity remains with you, and you will remain being their victim because your life has been changed by their wrongful deed against you.

It was actually the day of my Grandmother's funeral when I forgave the family member who had abused me as a child. At the time, I didn't even know I was still suffering from the effects. I was now twenty years old, and I very rarely even thought of him and the past in my day to day life. It had been fourteen years since I had last seen him. After the assault by the stranger had occurred, the police were called in to investigate. It was during lengthy police interviews that the reality of the long-term sexual abuse came to the surface. The police intervened and I never saw my abuser again.

I certainly didn't expect to react as I did when I saw him again at my Grandmother's funeral. Family and friends were gathered outside the chapel of rest, and as we began to walk inside following behind the coffin, I found myself stepping back. I was feeling hesitant and reluctant to stay with the immediate family. The thought of being so close to him filled me with terror. My throat felt dry, and I couldn't speak to take part in the service. My whole body was shaking.

Throughout the entire service, I just stood rigid on the spot and stared intensely at his back, but instead of seeing the tall looming monster figure that frightened me as a child, I saw an old broken man consumed by his grief.

## Forgiveness

I don't know where it came from or how it was even generated, but suddenly the thought swept into my consciousness: *Forgive him.* I shivered as I chased the thought away. *No, no I can't.* Seconds later as if to taunt me it came again, *Forgive him, Beverley.* I retaliated in a bid to put an end to my own foolishness, *No, no I won't, he doesn't deserve forgiveness.* Then came the final challenging thoughts: *If you love Lord Jesus as you say you do, you will forgive him.* I was stunned. I had caused a conflict within my own thoughts. I loved Jesus deeply and I wasn't prepared to let anything or anyone tarnish my love. I knew then I had to forgive this man to remain true and protect my own love.

It didn't come easily. I made several attempts to step forward as we all stood around the graveside but my legs just wouldn't move. I just couldn't do it. Eventually the mourners began to leave, and I knew it had to be done, as it was unlikely I'd ever see him again. I took a deep breath. *You can do this, Beverley, you can,* I reassured myself. I stepped forward and walked up to him. I stood on my tip-toes and kissed him on the cheek and I held his gaze - his eyes uninviting and cold, red-rimmed from his tears.

"*The past is the past,*" I told him. "*You are forgiven.*" Then I turned around and walked away.

I will always remember the feelings I had as I walked away. Never before had I ever experienced such an elated feeling. It was sudden and overpowering. I actually felt as if I could step up and walk on the air. The rush of peace flooded through my entire being. I felt as if the world had just opened up around me; I felt light and a softness folded around me. The song of the birds was delightful to my ears - the trees, the flowers and even the clouds in the sky looked so beautiful. I was free from the shadows of the past. Free from the burden of pain that I didn't even know had been trapped inside of me. I was finally free to live my life for the very first time.

It is not easy to forgive but we all have the ability to do so. Forgiveness is an act of free will. In life you are worthy of being free to love. Don't let someone who has hurt you, then also take from you your right to love. Open your heart and chase the shadows away by letting the light in.

When you are in the *Who Am I?* journey of your Spirit, Jesus teaches you the truth of your love by also allowing you to meet with your loved ones who have already passed over. You may also have Spiritual Guides. A Spiritual Guide can be one particular loved one, or he/she can also be a complete stranger, but they always have some kind of connection to you, whether from your own lifetime or even that of one of your ancestors. The point is that everything you hear or see in the Spirit, or a message given to you by means of Spiritual intervention, is important to you for your Spiritual growth, even if you are still within your physical life. If you are lucky enough to be given a message through a Spiritual Guide then don't hesitate to act upon it. It has been given to you to help you enrich your life, not hinder your existence.

After Death Experience<br>
**Go Into The Light**

## Forgiveness

I became of the Spirit within the Afterlife. There I found myself standing before Christ. We journeyed together through the heavens, and finally reached a place within the tunnel of life. On my right-hand side I could see the bright glowing light of a giant circle that seemed to be turning upon itself.

In the distance I saw the figure of a man, and as he neared me I realised I had never met him before, though I knew he had only just passed over into the Afterlife. He looked confused and I sensed he thought it was not yet his time to be here.

Then I heard Jesus whisper, "*Guide the Child of God home.*" And so I pointed to the glowing light and told the man, "*Go into the light and seek forgiveness from God.*"

Jesus then returned my Spirit back into my physical body and breathed life into me once again.

This particular ADE was one of hundreds that were all very similar, and every time I was always guiding others into the light. In essence I was being a Spiritual Guide to those who had just passed over, and although it may have appeared that I had no connection at all to these people, it would later transpire that my connection was in the ADE itself. These people within their physical lives had experienced an ADE, and previously been sent back. Now it was their turn to stay within the Afterlife to begin the *Who Am I?* journey of their Spirit with Jesus.

I have indeed had many ADEs in which I myself never actually went through the light. These were in essence exploring this earth, the old earth, and they do explain why many people can detect the *presence of Spirit* around them. I am not saying all such 'Spirit' walking this earth belong to living people having an ADE, as I did encounter many *lost souls*, most of whom I would just send to the light, but in the Spirit I was able to stroll along the beach and witness the events going on around certain people who were still of the living. I could never move anything that was physical. If a door was shut I couldn't open it by the handle, though I could just walk through it.

In the *Who Am I?* prophecies of Jesus, I write about these particular ADEs as being of *The Visitation of Christ*. Wherever I went Jesus was always with me. Whatever I saw He saw too. His visitation to man comes to me in the same understanding as His first visit to man 2000 years ago. The first time He came He was in His physical body and walked amongst man. Since 1987 He has been walking amongst man in His Spiritual body. It is a revelation that will change the world. The story of His visitation will explode onto the media platforms - engaging us all to a new higher consciousness, and social change. There are no secrets from God.

The following Actual Death Experience portrays a most unusual aspect of my ADEs, and although after 1992 I had many similar ones with another person, this particular one was the first of its kind. In essence Jesus had joined my Spirit with the Spirit of someone still within a physical life, and although the other person appeared unable to retain any memory of it, he did later go through all the emotional and physical changes that occur following an Actual Death Experience.

It occurred in 1988, when I encountered the Spirit of

Forgiveness

my husband David before we went our separate ways.

## After Death Experience
## **Cleansing Of The Spirit**

As I fell into the first folds of physical death, Jesus stood by my bedside waiting. He commanded my Spirit to rise up out of my physical body, and as I passed over into the Afterlife, I noticed I was now standing in my bedroom. I could see my physical body still lying within my bed, and next to me lay David's physical body.

I looked across the room, and there standing at the end of the bed I saw David's Spirit, and standing beside him I saw Jesus. I moved closer to David's Spirit and stood directly in front of him, while Jesus stood close by to my left-hand side.

Suddenly I saw the expression on David's face change, and he seemed to be experiencing pain. At that very moment, a gush of black murky liquid shot up towards the ceiling coming from behind David's Spirit.

Then I felt a sharp pain in the lower part of my spine, and as I looked up I saw the same murky liquid shoot up out from behind me.

Jesus raised His arms up into the air, and by a command the two streams of black liquid joined together above David's and my head. Then Jesus lowered His hands, and as He did the gushing stream of black liquid flowed out of the bedroom window.

Jesus then returned my Spirit back into my physical body and breathed life into me once again.

To write that this ADE changed our lives is an understatement. Following our recovery we were both physically and emotionally drained, and it took us both some time before we were able to get up out of bed. But it wasn't the physical aftermath that was consuming our thoughts. It was the emotional feelings we were both experiencing that had surfaced, and that we found ourselves talking about.

We were experiencing the *feeling of love* for one another. On that day, as we recovered, it was as if we were falling in love for the very first time. I felt proud of him and so happy to be in his life by his side, and he spoke of the same love for me.

The following weeks were just as enchanting. We laughed together. We joked together. We were happy together. It was an incredible feeling of contentment, which had been missing from our relationship for a very long time.

I never told David about the ADE, and I suspect on reflection that was a grave error of judgement on my part. Perhaps if I had explained such then our new revitalized relationship would have lasted the test of time. I waited for him to mention it and tell me what he experienced in it but he never did, and I couldn't understand why. Was he ashamed for not believing me when I first told him what was happening to me? Did he care that I needed him to help me through the ADEs? The seeds of doubt and suspicion were being slowly planted within our

## Forgiveness

relationship again; the negativity looming.

Within a few months we were arguing again. Doubting each other, and making accusations. This time there was no turning back, we were on the road to separation and divorce.

Unfortunately I didn't learn until 1992, after David and I had separated, that not everyone every time retains the memory of an Actual Death Experience. They can have all the physical and emotional changes caused by an ADE but not remember the actual experience itself.

## Author's Note

Sadly, in February 2010, my former husband David was diagnosed with Cancer, and seven months later on September 15th 2010, he passed over. We had been divorced for many years before his terminal illness, and our divorce proved bitter - creating many unpleasant memories.

Since David's passing, Jesus has taken my Spirit within several ADEs to be with David's Spirit. We have sat together and exchanged words of Spiritual love, forgiveness and protection for one another.

We Are Now Friends.

Forgiveness

## *Together We Shall Grow*

*Why will you not listen
When I ask you to hear?
Why will you not help me
When with you I am so near?
I desire God's forgiveness
This I need you to know
Let us help each other
And together we shall grow*

*When you look in the mirror
Tell me - who do you see?
Look close my friend
Your reflection is me*


*Together we shall grow - my Spirit and me*

# 6

# The Dancing Demons

The evil thought is as destructive to our Spiritual body as it is to our physical life. In the last chapter I wrote about forgiveness: how to learn within our physical lives to teach ourselves forgiveness before we pass over into the Afterlife, by instructing the Teacher of our thoughts to seek forgiveness from the people we have hurt, and forgiving those who have hurt us.

But what happens to those of us who can't or don't want to reach Spiritual forgiveness? Is there truly a way back for us eventually to reach paradise with Jesus?

Within my ADEs, Jesus taught me about what becomes of our Spirit if we live our physical lives with evil tendencies. He referred to these teachings as *'The Dancing Demons of the Evil Mind'*. These teachings reveal a shocking revelation, and I truly do pity anyone who finds the Dancing Demons as part of their Spiritual reality within the Afterlife.

Jesus' teachings were so horrifying; He took my Spirit in several stages to fully understand everything He was showing me.

The Dancing Demons

## After Death Experience
**Speak The Lord's Prayer**

I became of the Spirit within the Afterlife. There I found myself standing before Christ in a place that was not of this earth, the old earth, nor was it a place of the New Earth. I knew only that I was standing within the clouds in a place of reflection and knowledge.

Suddenly a huge creature appeared in front of me. It came quickly as if making an attempt to try and surprise me by its presence. It held no resemblance to a person, and although it wasn't tall it was wide in its figure. It had a head but its Spiritual body had no defined shape, so you could not see where its head joined its body. Its features were twisted, disjointed at every angle, and its Spiritual body was embedded with dark crusted scales. Its eyes were large, of different sizes, and out of proportion to the top half of its Spiritual body. They were black – reflecting pools of torment and pain.

I felt terror fill my senses at its mere presence, and the sight before me was so ugly I did not wish to look upon it, so I quickly turned my head away.

At that moment, Jesus commanded me to look, and so I had to turn my head back to gaze upon its foulness once again. A great fear swept over me for the darkness of the creature I was witnessing.

Jesus was stood to my left-hand side, and suddenly he commanded of me, "*Speak the Lord's Prayer*".

Immediately, I began to. The words flowed from my Spirit in haste, and at first the words came in jumbled sentences from the sheer fear I felt, but I did not dare to stop.

As I continued to recite the Lord's Prayer, I noticed that the creature then began to cower away, and retreat backwards.

Jesus then returned my Spirit back into my physical body and breathed life into me once again.

The only words to describe my reaction once I had recovered from this Actual Death Experience are those of experiencing the most terrifying anxiety and dread. How could something so gruesome actually exist? And why had Jesus allowed me to witness such? I was consumed with the mixed emotions of fright and heartbreak. How could my beautiful Lord Jesus have allowed such an ugly dark presence to come anywhere near me? Had I done something wrong and was He showing me what my Spirit would now become like? The memory of this ADE haunted my every waking moment. I was petrified and I desperately needed to understand it.

In another ADE of the same nature, Jesus took His teaching further.

## After Death Experience
### The Invisible Shield

I became of the Spirit within the Afterlife. There I found myself standing before Christ in a place that was

## The Dancing Demons

not of this earth, the old earth, nor was it a place of the New Earth. I knew only that I was standing within the clouds in a place of reflection and knowledge.

Once again, I saw a huge creature appear in front of me. Once again it came upon me suddenly, as if trying to approach without detection. It looked as horrific as the first one had, with the same features. And once again, a feeling of a great fear swept over me.

Jesus was stood to my left-hand side, and this time I instantly began to speak the Lord's Prayer. Once again the words came from me in jumbled sentences. The fear was overpowering.

Suddenly Jesus lifted up His arm, and with a command of His hand He placed an invisible shield to surround my entire Spirit.

Jesus then returned my Spirit back into my physical body and breathed life into me once again.

I wish I could say that the memory of seeing Jesus place an invisible shield around my Spirit made this ADE easier to comprehend, but it didn't. He was showing me, as He had once promised my Spirit, that I had nothing to be afraid of because I was protected by Him, but even the knowledge of His protection didn't ease my fear.

In ADEs that followed Jesus began to explain His teachings to me. *"The child you have encountered by my will is the Spirit of the evil mind. The Spirit absorbs the darkness of its wrongful deeds. The plagues of the Spiritual body have no place in my Father's kingdom."*

## After Death Experience
### The Dancing Demons of the Evil Mind

I became of the Spirit within the Afterlife. There I found myself standing before Christ, as before in a place that was not of this earth, the old earth, nor was it a place of the New Earth. I knew only that I was standing within the clouds in a place of reflection and knowledge.

Once again I saw a huge gruesome creature appear in front of me. I stood trembling at the mere sight of it, and instantly I began speaking the Lord's Prayer.

Jesus was stood to my left-hand side, He raised His hand and made a command, placing the invisible shield to surround my entire Spirit.

This time, as I stood witnessing the presence of the evil Spirit before me, I noticed several large gargoyle-like creatures jumping up and down upon the evil Spirit. As each of the creatures jumped mid-air, they opened their mouths to expose large sharp pointed fangs, and as they landed back down upon the evil Spirit, they each bit into their host. With each bite the evil Spirit roared out in sheer agony.

Suddenly one of the gargoyle-like creatures noticed my Spirit, and it flew through the air towards me in an attempt to land on my Spirit. In an instant it bounced off the invisible shield, which sent it hurtling backwards midair.

Jesus then returned my Spirit back into my physical

body and breathed life into me once again.

In ADEs that followed Jesus explained His teachings to me: *"You have witnessed in my presence the Dancing Demons of the Evil Mind. Those who nurture evil thoughts within their lives are feeding the demons that bring the plagues of their sinful acts. Go and tell all of what you have witnessed, as with all things living, the starvation of food will bring the end of life."*

When Jesus spoke of the demons' food, He is referring to the evil thought. If you live your physical life nurturing evil thoughts, you are in essence supplying a demon with nourishment, which not only provides it with existence but also gives it growth, and the stronger the demon becomes the more power it has over your Spiritual existence. In essence its negative energy absorbs all negativity. The only way to ensure you do not create a demon awaiting your Spiritual birth is to live your physical life without evil thoughts.

In May 1992, Jesus joined my Spirit with the Spirit of another living person. His name is Trevor Enstone, and this was the second time I had encountered the Spirit of another living person within my ADEs. The first ADE was the time He had joined my Spirit with the Spirit of my former husband David in 1988; however, with David it was only the one ADE. The ADE's with Trevor Enstone's Spirit were frequent, occurring between May 1992 and February 1993, then again on one occasion in April 2012, which was the last time I encountered his Spirit in an ADE.

Although I did not begin to pen the *Who Am I?*

Prophecies of Jesus until 1993 (till 1996), I did not fully understand the reason for my Spiritual union with Trevor Enstone's Spirit. Even in 2008 when it was finally revealed within my testimonial to the Churches, I still couldn't grasp the importance of what was happening.

*Extracts, (Page 9 of 139) - Written and Accepted Testimonial*

"*In His journey with my Spirit, Jesus has made me a living witness to the Revelations of St John, but as I have told you, I am not alone as His witness, as there is another like me. His name is Trevor Enstone I can do no more than to give you my promise that every word upon these pages is the truth in the name of God, and declare here without fear that factual proof will be put before you to prove Jesus' journey of my Spirit, and Roger's Spirit, and from such all doubt shall be washed away and the thoughts of man shall be cleansed to honour these words of truth.*

*The Revelations of St John have indeed come to pass. Man will rejoice and become of great celebration for a forthcoming future of peace within mankind. My Spirit with Trevor Enstone's Spirit has walked upon the New Earth with Christ Our Lord, Our Master, Our Teacher and Our Protector. And also I make claim that my Spirit with Trevor Enstone's Spirit has seen a Great Golden Stairway descend down from the New Heaven with Christ Our Lord, Our Master, Our Teacher and Our Protector.*

*And from this claim the Nations of Man shall rejoice, and they will come together in honour of God Our Heavenly Father. And they who rejoice in Him shall put down their weapons of war and destruction, and declare peace amongst themselves.*

*And the children of our bodies shall have returned the*

## The Dancing Demons

*beauty of their innocence. And the Monarch of this great country will be restored to its former glory. And the flames of a Great Fire of Love will burn brightly in the hearts of all those who have not fallen away from God. And new flames of a Great Fire of Love will burn brightly in the hearts of those who have fallen away from God when within their hearts they desire to see the light of God.*

*With open eyes that see and ears that hear it will be verified to all that no living man or woman could ever put this testimonial together by their own hand. For this is the labour of God's love bestowed upon us all."*

The greatest hardships I experienced during the *Who Am I?* journey of my Spirit was learning to understand the full extent of what my ADEs revealed, and their purpose. I understood they were bringing a message of hope, and a promise of a forthcoming peace amongst mankind; but I could not fully appreciate the true scale of the change that would occur. Within my ADEs Jesus spoke of a Spiritual Awakening - a sudden change in Consciousness that would bring about a freedom from Spiritual and Social domination, in essence to free the suppressed. But before we can be truly awakened, we have to understand our Spiritual existence within the Afterlife. Once we understand the true meaning of our own *Free Will* and acknowledge the consequences in generating negative energy that arise from having evil thoughts - then we will be able to make the much needed changes to our physical lives on a conscious level.

Jesus' teachings of the Dancing Demons of the Evil Mind prove that our future Spiritual existence is in our own hands. We can choose to be good. We can choose to be bad. The choice is ours to make. Within our physical lives we can hide behind a mask of pretence; we can live our lives thinking evil thoughts and hiding them away from other people. But in the Spirit there is no mask to hide behind. The truth of how you conducted your physical life is visible to everyone you encounter within the Afterlife.

Many people will often excuse their behaviour by the existence of 'a devil' - giving it a separate and powerful identity, and then using the excuse that they were innocent of the evil deed as they were controlled by this devil. Within my ADEs Jesus shows that we are in control of our thoughts, and the only way evil has dominion over our physical lives is when we surrender that control to the evil thought.

My ADE encounters with Trevor Enstone's Spirit came to show how a man can change his Spiritual existence by changing his own thought process within his physical life. This particular ADE occurred in May 1992, two weeks after I began a physical relationship with him.

## After Death Experience
### The Birth of His Spirit

I became of the Spirit within the Afterlife. There I found myself standing before Christ in a place that I knew was of this earth, the old earth.

Jesus was to my left-hand side, and I saw that we were standing at the bottom of a bed within a bedroom.

## The Dancing Demons

There I saw the figure of someone within the bed, and the bedroom door was to my right-hand side.

Jesus raised up His hand and made a command, and in that instant I saw the Spirit of Trevor Enstone rise up out of the figure within the bed. As his Spirit rose up I heard him call out the name of a woman, but I knew it was not my name.

Suddenly my attention was drawn to the far left-hand corner of the room. Near to the ceiling I saw a nest, and inside the nest I saw a large gargoyle-like creature awakening. It glared down at my Spirit and in an instant flew out of the nest and down towards my Spirit.

I sensed the creature was confused by my presence, and it attempted to attack me. I turned round and fled through the bedroom door, and the creature chased after me but it was not able to land upon my shoulders.

Jesus then returned my Spirit back into my physical body and breathed life into me once again.

The presence of a demon at Trevor Enstones Spiritual birth indicated that within his physical life he was a man who had nurtured bad thoughts. However, at the time I did not fully understand Jesus' teachings of the Dancing Demons. My lack of understanding for His teachings would later seal my understanding as to Trevor Enstone's physical life.

In the ADEs that followed during which I encountered Trevor Enstone's Spirit, which can only be described as a *Spiritual Courtship*, I saw his essence to be of a great beauty. His Spirit was tall and handsome, and he appeared youthful. In my understanding at the time, I knew only that if he was a bad man then I would have seen such reflecting in his Spirit. In truth, my fear for the ADEs prevented me from understanding the teachings Jesus was giving me.

I should have been concentrating more during my physical life of what our two Spirits were doing within this Spiritual Courtship but my thoughts were consumed by the Spiritual union itself. I had been waiting five years, (since 1987) to find out the reason for my ADEs, and now suddenly I was encountering the Spirit of another living person within them, and I came to believe that he would know the reason for my ADEs.

During the following ADEs concerning this Spiritual Courtship, my Spirit with Trevor Enstone's Spirit were being united to perform a Stage Play. It was the story of the Two Witnesses, (Rev 11), and the Woman and the Dragon (Rev 12). The Stage Play was to be performed upon the New Earth in front of an audience of people belonging to that earth. Within these particular ADEs our two Spirits explored theatres, and we visited a dome-shaped theatre within New York City upon the New Earth. Then we were shown an open air theatre in which the play was to be staged.

Within my physical life during this time, I penned everything that I was experiencing and titled the work as The *Who Am I?* Stage Play. In Revelation 12 – concerning the Woman and the Dragon - the woman is pregnant and later she gives birth to the child in the Spirit. In the Spiritual Courtship, I became pregnant in my Spirit, and the pregnancy in the Spirit kept causing my physical body to change in its natural shape. But unlike a normal pregnancy, where the physical body changes over a period of time, the Spiritual pregnancy was causing my physical body to change shape suddenly within a matter of minutes in front of many witnesses. My normal size was a dress size 10 to 12, with a flat abdomen and a slim waist. Within minutes my physical body would take on the shape of a heavily pregnant woman in the last stages of labour. On countless occasions I was rushed up to the local hospital and prepared for what appeared to be a normal birth - only then to have the many doctors and nurses left perplexed by the absence of a physical baby. Finally, in February 1993, my Spirit gave birth to a child in the Spirit, and my physical body never changed in shape again.

In an ADE following the birth of the child in the Spirit, I had an encounter with Trevor Enstone's Spirit that appeared to bring an end to our Spiritual Courtship, and the Stage Play.

## After Death Experience
**Swallowed by the Mouth of Darkness**

I became of the Spirit within the Afterlife. There I found myself standing before Christ in a place that was not of this earth, the old earth, nor was it a place of the New Earth. I knew only that I was standing within the clouds in a place of reflection and knowledge.

There I stood with Jesus on my left-hand side, and

Trevor Enstone's Spirit was standing on my right-hand side.

In the distance I saw what seemed like a tremendous dark cloud, like a giant tornado raging towards us at a great speed destroying everything within its path. It roared towards us echoing the sounds of an almighty deafening thunder, and it was far darker, far louder than anything my Spirit had ever seen or heard before. As it neared, I saw it appeared to have a huge wide mouth, and it seemed to take the position of being below to where we were standing.

Suddenly Trevor Enstone's Spirit stepped forward, and in that very moment I saw the mouth of darkness swallow up his Spirit. I heard his Spirit call out in great pain, as the force sucked his Spirit up into an endless darkness. Then I saw his Spirit holding out his arms towards me, and I heard him cry out the words, "Help me!" I stood watching helplessly, and then I heard my Spirit shout down to his Spirit, *"Don't worry, Trevor, I will save you!"*

I reached down and grasped hold of his hand. Then I pulled with all my might trying to bring him out of the darkness. The force crushed my hand and I could feel the pain running up my arm; and as I pulled I began speaking out the words to the Lord's Prayer, but no matter how hard I tried, I could not free him from the darkness.

Jesus then returned my Spirit back into my physical body and breathed life into me once again.

I often found myself questioning this particular

## The Dancing Demons

ADE, especially as to why I had called out to his Spirit that I would save him when I knew salvation only came through Jesus. At the time of its occurrence, I thought his Spirit had stepped out into the path of the darkness to prevent it from swallowing up my Spirit, and I thought it was a warning that within his physical life he was in great danger, as the darkness had appeared so quickly.

It later turned out that it wasn't my Spirit the darkness had come for. In the latter months of 1992, unbeknown to me, Trevor Enstone within his physical life had begun having the most horrendous evil thoughts. So consumed with hate and bitterness that he soon began acting upon them, and he began living his physical life committing criminal acts. They resulted in him going to prison on two separate occasions, and his physical life was never the same again. His beautiful Spirit had been lost to a force of darkness.

On reflection, many readers will probably think that the presence of the demon at his Spiritual birth should have acted as a forewarning to me. And in a sense they would be correct to believe such, because I now have the same thoughts. But it is easy to think differently afterwards when you have more knowledge, and understand the teachings of Jesus.

If you find yourself living your physical life with evil thoughts, be prepared for the consequences within your Spiritual growth - even if your thoughts within your physical life are never discovered. In the Spirit it does not matter if you have acted upon the thoughts or not - the thoughts are all you need to nourish a demon. However, if you were once the *thinker of evil deeds* but you have now changed your ways and you no longer live with such darkness, then by your own free will you have liberated your Spirit of its presence for your Spiritual growth.

In April of 2012, I found myself standing in the Spirit within an ADE observing the tornado of darkness again, and I knew Trevor Enstone's Spirit was still caught up inside it. Jesus then stepped forward and I heard Him say,

*"Be gone with you now, Child."*

On hearing His command I left, and since then I've never seen the darkness or encountered Trevor Enstone's Spirit again.

## The Dancing Demons

### As I Stand

*If I were a Lawyer*
*I would stand for the truth*
*If he whom I represented were of untruth*
*Then I would sentence him myself*

*'A fool!' I hear them cry*
*'For where there is the truth*
*There is also the untruth*
*And thou shall have less*
*If the one of truth come not to thee'*

*To them I say this:*
*'The fool is not I*
*But of the man*
*Who comes to me with the untruth'*

# 7

## Paradise

Jesus' teaching to the Churches pertaining to my Testimonial
*"Believe not this woman her truth, and you do no more than take the babe from out of the stable and place him in the walls of a Palace."*

There shall be no atom bomb for His earth. This is the promise of Jesus made within my Actual Death Experiences. He then instructed me to write down everything I heard within a letter and send it to the Churches on my recovery from the ADE. I did, and the letter formed two pages of direct explanations for the purpose of my ADEs, and His promises, one of which being: *It is written within the Lord's Prayer - It shall be done on earth as it is in heaven.*

The latter is referring to His *Who Am I?* journey of the Spirit. Everyone meets with Christ when we pass over into the Afterlife, and we all have a one to one relationship with Him, as He takes us on the *Who Am? I* journey of our Spirit. In my case I was still living a physical life during Jesus' *Who Am I?* journey of my Spirit, and so it has indeed been done on earth as it is in Heaven.

## Paradise

Over the years I have grown significantly. I have now reached a level of a higher consciousness in a most incredible Spiritual Awakening.

I have gone from being a trembling wreck in fear of my ADEs to having trust for His teachings. I have gone from dreading the ADE as it begins to being now able to call out His name the moment my Spirit rises up from out of my physical body. I have gone from believing I had a 'right' to walk by His side, and without realisation putting my foot ahead of His (see ADE - The Marble Steps), to now falling to my knees in His presence, bowing my head respectfully.

It is only after you have been able to evaluate the purpose of Jesus' *Who Am I?* Journey of the Spirit, and realise the reason for His new Spiritual Teachings, that you can truly appreciate the miracle that has been upon us since 1987.

Many people may ask: 'Why did Jesus come in His Spiritual body to walk amongst men in His vistation of man, and not a physical body so we could all see Him?' The answer is because of what we have become within our physical lives: how we conduct ourselves, and how the world today is as it is.

We have caused war and destruction for want of power and self-righteous belief. We use religion as a weapon. We turn upon our brothers and sisters. We disregard human life. We use the planet's resources to the point of no return for nature, for wildlife. The list is endless. But over all, it is everything we do that is not good. Try and imagine honestly what we would do to

Jesus if He were to appear within a physical body. If He came with His Spiritual teachings to show us how to reach a state of higher consciousness in preparation for our transition onto the New Earth? Would Jesus truly be able to walk amongst us without the interference of the Governments or the Churches? And what about in general? Would everyone allow Him to walk freely amongst us with His Spiritual teachings without someone somewhere wanting to go down in history as being the one who killed Jesus.

In our world today, government officials have to have their bodyguards and a system of tight security. The shooting of JF Kennedy gives a clear example of a successful assassination, alongside other unsuccessful attempts on high figures, such as that on His Holiness Pope John Paul II. The Pope himself is no longer able to walk freely amongst the people without a high level of security in place. Within our world we have indeed created an impossible situation that would not allow Jesus to walk in peace amongst us whether we are rich or poor or of commoner or royal birth.

Jesus' new Spiritual teachings do not countenance any exceptions. He teaches that it is wrong to kill – to take the life of another person. It does not matter who we are or what are the circumstances, it is wrong and against God's essence of love to commit murder. This includes the practice of the *death penalty*. What would the governments of the countries that still use the death penalty as a means of punishment do if they were told to stop. Would they consider Jesus as anti-government, and therefore dismiss His presence and refuse His Spiritual teachings.

## Paradise

When we acknowledge the *Who Am I?* prophecies of Jesus, and accept His Spiritual lessons, it becomes clear that He is teaching us all to become of a higher consciousness for life, showing us that we are each our own 'Teacher' within our physical lives. We each have the opportunity of free will, and when we value that gift our deeds are within our control. Once we learn how to open our higher consciousness, we will generate a wave of positive energy in a new Spiritual Awakening, and we will then have evolved as a species. The reward is peace amongst mankind, and the ability to transcend to the New Earth – once we pass over into the Afterlife.

In essence He is teaching us that we do indeed have the ability to live together as a human race in peace and harmony. We do not have to rage war upon one another, and we do not have to base our survival on a way of life that is destroying our planet. We have to take responsibility for how our world has become today, and realise the only way we can make much needed changes and create a better world to live in is to learn how to open our higher consciousness.

The existence of the New Earth has often been a subject of debate. Some religious houses consider it as being of this earth in the future, after it has been cleansed by God of everything that is immoral. Others speculate that it is a future earth yet to be created. In His Spiritual teachings Jesus brings the revelation that the New Earth is indeed already in existence. It is not of this earth (the old earth), nor is it of an existence yet to be created. The New Earth is where the *Throne* of Jesus sits, and where we are all the Children of God. The men are all considered to be *kings,* and Jesus is the King of all Kings.

Within His *Who Am I?* journey with my Spirit, Jesus has lifted the veil of His great mystery to reveal an understanding for the scriptures and the book of Revelation. He brings a new hope after all hope has been lost. He brings validation for God's promise to restore faith. He brings understanding for our resurrection. Most importantly, He brings us awareness both of our existence, and of our shortcomings.

Within my ADEs, Jesus carried my Spirit to walk with Him upon the New Earth. It was the second time I was allowed to meet with the Spirit of my late father, John Gilmour.

## Actual Death Experience
### Central Park - New York

In the Spirit I became and Lord Jesus carried my Spirit away to walk with Him upon the New Earth.

There I stood in the Spirit in recognition of my surroundings, as my entire being filled with a sense of familiarity. The place I knew it to be was Central Park in the City of New York in the United States of America.

And I was surrounded by both narrow and tall trees and short and thick trees. And every leaf upon every branch within this place glowed in every shade of leafy green known to man, and in many other shades of colours never before seen by him.

In front of me I saw a lake, and the surface of the water sparkled brightly like a beautiful diamond glistening under the ray of light; and I was to know that the water was rich – bathed with the richness of life.

The verges were of the greenest grass I had ever seen, and a silvery hue simmered at the tip of each blade of grass. Dotted within the grass, I saw clusters of tiny flowers, and their deep colours of yellow, blue, purple and white reflected within the silvery tinge.

In the distance, I saw an opening between the trees, and standing slightly behind one of the trees I saw the tall figure of a man. As I looked closer, I saw it was the Spirit of my late father John Gilmour, and my entire senses filled with joy. I noticed his facial appearance and stature was that of his thirties within his physical life. Then I noticed he was pointing across to his right-hand side.

To my left-hand side I saw the Spirit of Trevor Enstone standing tall and proud, and his facial features were handsome and pleasing to the eye. I tugged at his arm, as I became overwhelmed with the desire to show him that my dad's Spirit was standing by the tree. But as I did so, I looked up and noticed that his gaze was fixed, staring intently at something to his left.

I looked over at my dad's Spirit again and then across to my left-hand side following his pointed finger.

There I saw the sky opening, dividing in two; and as the two parts of the sky opened, a great golden stairway began descending down from out of the sky before positioning itself in mid-air. The golden stairs were encrusted with precious stones, each of them radiating brightly in glowing opulent colours. The sight before me was of such grandeur that I was held captive by its presence.

Then I noticed a figure standing on the third golden step from the bottom. I looked closely, and it was the Spirit of my late father John Gilmour, but his appearance and stature were those of the age of fifty-two – the age at which he passed over into the Afterlife.

I saw him tug at his trousers, a familiar gesture he always made within his physical life for not wearing a belt. Then he lifted up his left hand and began waving towards me. His face glowed with happiness. He beamed a smile of contentment, and all around me I felt the presence of Angels and I knew my dad's Spirit was now in the presence of God as he stood upon the great golden stairway of the New Heaven.

Jesus then returned my Spirit back into my physical body and breathed life into me once again.

On my recovery after this ADE, I was held in a state of sheer confusion. I could not understand why or indeed how it was possible that I had witnessed my dad's Spirit in two different positions within the same ADE, and especially why I had seen him in two totally different appearances.

In following ADEs, Jesus explained His teaching. When my dad's Spirit had finished his *Who Am I?* journey with Jesus, His Spiritual body was given a new life, and from such he passed over onto the New Earth which became his home. His Spiritual body now bore the resemblance of a man in his thirties, as within his *Who Am I?* Journey he had realised in his truth that this was the happiest time of his physical incarnation. His actual Spirit, however, retained the same appearance as when he had passed over into the Afterlife and had accended up to the New Heaven.

## Actual Death Experience
### The Bumble Bees Do Not Sting Here

In the Spirit I became and Lord Jesus carried my Spirit away to walk with Him upon the New Earth.

Jesus stood to my left-hand side, and I found myself within some place of the most stunning countryside.

There I stood at the edge of a huge meadow, and a feeling of pure peacefulness filled my entire being, as if I had been suddenly wrapped up in a warm blanket. It was breathtakingly beautiful, and there seemed to be no end to the vast landscape. I sensed a feeling of belonging and joy, an ecstatic sense of happiness for being there.

I saw the grass had grown to quite a height, and I suddenly wanted to run through the field and trail my hand through the long stems of grass. Its colour was striking – a beautiful vivid green, and it swayed gently as if caught up in a gentle breeze. In between the tall blades of grass, I saw small gatherings of flowers. The colours were incredibly bright, gleaming intensely with an exquisite radiance.

In that moment, as the longing to run on through the field swept over me, I became aware that I was barefoot, and I sensed a strong feeling of hesitation in the presence of bees fostering the flowers. What if I stood on one and it stung me, I suddenly thought in my new-found reluctance.

Then Jesus stepped forward and said, "*The Bumble Bees do not sting here.*"

Jesus then returned my Spirit back into my physical body and breathed life into me once again.

Indeed, in my many ADEs upon the New Earth, Jesus was revealing its great magnificence. I witnessed cars being driven along without any fumes. I saw tall skyscrapers among which I was able to fly up and stand on the rooftops, looking out across at the vast scenery: the revelation of many great cities which I knew existed upon the old earth, places where even the buildings appeared to be enriched with the essence of life; fields, parks, flourishing rivers with fish in abundance.

I encountered people of all different ages, and nationalities, heard the laughter of children playing, the sound of music and celebrations; the galloping of horses. I saw the most glorious sandy beaches. A world where, although people were busy within their own lives, nothing was rushed. All people had time for one another. There was no sadness, there were no tears, no arguments or fears, and every day felt like a beautiful summer's day.

In one particular Actual Death Experience, Jesus

showed me the reason why no confrontations happened upon the New Earth.

### Actual Death Experience
### Leave Me of Your Company

Into the Spirit I became, and Lord Jesus carried my Spirit away to walk with Him upon the New Earth.

Jesus was stood to my left-hand side, and I found myself standing next to a very long table covered in a white table cloth. I was busy preparing the table for a feast of celebration.

In the distance I saw the Spirit of a woman walking towards me, and when she reached me, I realised I had never met her before.

The woman began speaking to me, and although she was polite and respectful in manner, I noticed her words did not rest easily with me, as she was not communicating an understanding for my love; she was speaking differently about the love I represented and believed in.

Suddenly, I heard myself saying to her, "*Leave me of your company.*"

As soon as I said these words, she could no longer speak to me, and she had to walk away and leave me be.

Jesus then returned my Spirit back into my physical

body and breathed life into me once again.

This ADE revealed that whereas the people upon the New Earth have different views and opinions, if their love is not the same as yours they cannot remain in your company once you have asked them to leave.

Can you imagine how enriched our physical lives would become if we could just learn this one simple code of conduct! Racism on all levels would no longer exist. General disagreements which result in people hurting each other would come to an end. We can still have debates amongst ourselves but not to the point of causing offence and generating a negative energy.

## Actual Death Experience
### Have You Heard of Nostradamus?

Into the Spirit I became, and Lord Jesus carried my Spirit away to walk with Him upon the New Earth.

Jesus was stood to my left-hand side, and I found myself standing in front of a building that appeared to be old, as it had vines growing up its walls. It appeared to be the type of house that would have been built in England's 1920s. Although it seemed to be an old building, and I sensed no one lived there, every brick radiated the essence of life. The building itself felt alive. It seemed to emanate love – almost as if it were emitting the love all its previous owners had held for it. At that moment I suddenly knew it was the old Railway House. It was as if the house itself had told me of its existence.

## Paradise

In the distance I saw the Spirit of a woman walking towards me, and when she reached me, I realised I had never met her before.

Suddenly I heard myself asking her, *"Where are we?"*

The woman smiled warmly, and in answer to my question she replied, *"Have you not heard of Nostradamus?"*

Before I could reply, Jesus stepped forward and He said to the woman, *"She is not to know of such things yet."*

On hearing Jesus' words, the woman bowed respectfully towards Him, and began to step away backwards, for she knew it was wrong to turn her back upon Him.

Jesus then returned my Spirit back into my physical body and breathed life into me once again.

After my recovery from this ADE, I had a sense of confusion as I had never heard the word Nostradamus before. But in a friendly conversation with my neighbour soon after, although I did not speak about my ADEs, I did casually ask her if she knew the meaning of the word Nostradamus. It was she who then told me who Nostradamus was, and in the following weeks I found myself at the local library reading as many books as I could find about him. Over the years I began to realise that some of his quatrains seemed to have a direct link to my Actual Death Experiences, and Jesus' *Who Am I? Journey of my Spirit*, especially the ones that predict the coming of a new Spiritual Leader within the 21st Century.

It has to be remembered that Jesus has been walking amongst man within His Spiritual body most certainly since 1987, when my ADEs first began, to the present day.

Nostradamus describes an Eastern teacher who strikes at the world. He may use unusual and unorthodox devices to stir people up, disturbing the status 'codes' of social and religious behaviour in our materialistic times. In this sense Jesus is indeed a teacher who has risen from the East, and His new Spiritual teachings within His *Who Am I?* prophecies are very forthright and enlightening. It should also be remembered that Jesus validates the life of Michel de Nostredame, and therefore also his works, by permitting his name to be spoken as it was within His presence.

When I began writing the *Who Am I?* Prophecies of Jesus, I often found myself automatically using a style of verse to explain the ADE, and the teaching behind it. And although the verses were not as complex as the quatrains penned by Nostradamus, many of them certainly had an "old-worldly" feel about them, and they always held a hidden meaning.

## *Thoughts*

*What are these thoughts that surround me?*
*The visions that dance through my head.*
*Let me show you the world, I encounter*
*When I am alone in my bed.*

*Break - free from this life that enchains me*
*From those oblivious to my Soul.*
*Break - free, and ride a cloud into the night.*
*And to my friend, my Spirit I behold.*

## 8

## Living With Chronic Actual Death Experiences

### Part One

The fostering glint of empathy reflected genuinely in Dr Franklin's eyes.

*"How are you feeling today?"* she asked. Her tone was mixed with both acceptance and hope. I was on one of my regular monthly visits at her surgery.

I sat rigid on the chair opposite her, my entire body motionless. I could not even tilt my head. The fierce burning pain surged ruthlessly over the crown of my head, and flowed down the back towards my brain-stem. Then on impact the acute pain exploded into a shower of intense heat, covering my entire head in a blanket of sharp prickly pins and needles.

The constant burning pain didn't subside. In the very moment the eruption occurred, it triggered the surging pain to emanate over the crown of my head again. I was totally exhausted. The intense pain was only the tip of the iceberg. I was also sleep deprived, and not just by a couple of restless nights, my insomnia was infinite. I had not had a natural sleep since 1992, when my ADEs had opened on a whole new level because my brain just didn't function like a normal person's.

Sometimes I felt as if the constant burning sensation was the only thing that kept me going, kept me alive. How ironic it all seemed: the only time I had any liberation from the physical agony keeping me alive was when I was experiencing death in an Actual Death Experience. I was free from all the pain during my ADEs.

Dr Franklin sat patiently waiting for me to speak. I smiled weakly.

*"I'm struggling. The pain is pretty bad today. Other than that there has been no change in my ADEs."*

My voice quivered from the force of the pain, and I felt the tears threatening to gush from my eyes. I glanced down in a bid to avoid detection but it was too late; Dr Franklin was already reaching over to hand me a paper tissue from out of the handkerchief box on her desk.

She stood up and came over to me and helped me to my feet. Then she gave me a reassuring hug.

*"It's going to be all right. One day the medical world will understand your Actual Death Experiences,"* she said confidently. No one had ever heard of a medical case such as mine before, so knowledge as to how to treat my condition was non-existent.

Dr Franklin herself could only prescribe me with a range of medication that she hoped would help suppress the symptoms for both the pain and the insomnia. I also suffered from a sensitivity to 'bright light' and I could not be in a room or a car when the radio was on, due to the frequency output. In appreciating my sensitivity to bright light, Dr Franklin would always turn down the lights in her surgery and close the window shutters in preparation for my consultation. Her professionalism and consideration for me was such a huge relief, especially when you take into account how little the medical sector knew about ADEs.

I gently lifted the over-sized hood of my coat over my head to cover my eyes. It was sometimes the only way I could go outside in the daylight, unless I wore my sunglasses. I sighed wearily as I prepared to walk out into the main public area of the practice. It was not going to be easy. The constant burning sensation in my head would sometimes also react towards the 'thoughts' of other people around me, mainly because the Higher Consciousness – the Spiritual Mind – communicates on a telepathic level, and sometimes when this happened to me it proved utterly ghastly.

I was so lucky to have found Dr Franklin. Over the years, not every medical professional whom I have encountered has shown the same level of care towards me, and this has been difficult, causing all sorts of problems as a result of silly presumptions, to the point of costing me my children, my home, and even my career as a children's authoress.

I have been having the ADEs since 1987, but before 1992 I didn't have the constant burning pain in my head, and I was able to rest and fall asleep naturally. I still suffered with the light and radio sensitivity, and the limbs in my body were always stiff straight after an ADE, but I managed to live a reasonably normal life. I was only having the Actual Death Experiences about once every two to three months (except in the very first week), and so once I had recovered from the ADE, I would have the weeks in between to get on with my life.

The only time my ADEs stopped completely was during both my pregnancies. Oliver was born in 1989, and Westley was born in 1991. There was one exception when I was eight months pregnant with Oliver. I had thought I'd stopped having the ADEs completely - convinced they were now over, and I wouldn't have another one. But then one night I had one right out of the blue. This ADE shook me to the core, and it was to be the beginning of the medical world finding out about my condition.

## Actual Death Experience
**Where Is My Baby?**

As I fell into the first moments of this physical death, my Spirit rose up out of my body and I became of the Afterlife.

I hovered in mid-air above my physical body lying upon my bed. Then I saw a small glowing circle of light appear next to my bedroom window. It vibrated intensely, spinning around upon itself. Suddenly it darted forwards and shot out of the closed bedroom window; the ball of light held itself in the air, as if beckoning me to follow it.

I floated towards the window and passed through it into the open. Then I reached out to touch the ball of light, and as I held it in my hand, I felt myself rushing forwards and upwards.

The wind brushed against my face as I flew through the air. The ball of light took me, lightening the darkness around me as I shot swiftly through the darkened sky.

In the distance I saw another much bigger glowing light, and I could feel myself being pulled towards it. I sensed I was drifting down a long tunnel. Then as the ball of light in my hand merged with the light at the end of the tunnel, a sudden vivid white brightness surrounded me.

In every direction I was surrounded by the vibrant brightness. I felt the familiar feeling of peace engulf my senses, and I sensed Jesus standing beside me and to my left-hand side.

Suddenly, I looked down upon myself, and I saw that my abdomen was flat, and I heard myself call out to Jesus,

*"Where is my baby?"*

Jesus then returned my Spirit back into my physical body and breathed life into me once again.

When I recovered from this ADE, I cradled my pregnancy bump as a feeling of anxiety swept over me.

## Living With Chronic Actual Death Experiences

*Why had I not been able to see my baby? What did it mean? Was Jesus showing me that I was going to lose my baby? Is that why I was no longer able to see my bump?* The nagging thoughts taunted me, and I could feel my heartbeat racing. I moved my hand over my bump desperately wanting to feel my baby move, but there was nothing.

*Something is wrong with my baby, I know there is!*

I glanced across at my husband David, who was sleeping soundly. I knew I had to go to the hospital but I couldn't wake him to explain just why. David didn't understand my ADEs, and I knew he would be angry if I woke him to tell him I'd just had one.

I slipped out of the bed and crept out of the bedroom, then I telephoned for a taxi before throwing on an overcoat. The tears streamed down my face as I sat in the back of the taxi, my hands shaking from the dread of my thoughts as I still hadn't felt my baby move.

Once inside the hospital, I made my way up the empty, dimly lit corridor to the nurses' reception area. The constant flow of my tears had begun to make my head hurt, but the banging thud in my head was the least of my worries.

Suddenly I felt an arm around me. I glanced up and saw a nurse standing next to me.

*"Are you all right?"* Her tone was concerned. I shook my head to answer her *'No'*.

*"What has happened to get you in such a state?"* she

asked as she walked me towards the reception desk.

I couldn't tell her I'd had an ADE. What would she think of me if I did? The words slipped out before I could stop them as I muttered nervously,

*"I've just had a bad dream and now I can't feel my baby move."*

The nurse reassured me that everything would be all right, and moments later she had me strapped to a heartbeat monitor. Within minutes we could hear the loud thudding of my baby's heartbeat.

*"See, I told you everything would be all right,"* the nurse smiled.

I closed my eyes as the relief flooded through me and the anxiety from the ADE subsided.

I was kept in hospital for the rest of the night and scheduled to see my Gynaecologist, Dr Brent, that morning. But as I waited for my appointment I could feel the anxiety rising again: *What if I have another ADE while I am pregnant? What will happen to my baby?* Once again the questioning thoughts were tormenting me, and by the time I went in to see Dr Brent I was in a terrible state.

This time I knew I had to explain myself, no matter how odd or crazy it sounded. It wasn't as if I could control the ADEs, and I didn't enjoy having them, so it wasn't really my fault and I didn't know why they were happening. I had just resigned myself to the fact they had become part of my life, and after they had stopped eight months before, I'd thought they had ended.

Dr Brent listened to my story attentively. I was half expecting him to stop me in mid-sentence to tell me I was being silly, or worse, that I was obviously suffering from some form of mental illness. But he never did. Even though I explained the ADEs, I never revealed that it was Jesus whom I was always encountering. I don't know why I remained silent about Jesus, but I suspect it was because in the early years of my ADEs, I never thought of Jesus' presence in them as being of any significant importance. I had actually placed more worth on the fact that I had encountered my dad's Spirit, and the Spirit of the late Cary Grant, the famous Hollywood actor.

After hearing about my ADEs (*at the time I called them NDEs - Near death Experiences*), Dr Brent left the room, and when he returned he'd made his decision.

*"I think it best if I were to induce your baby. We don't know what the side effects are in this case, so it is better to be safe than sorry."*

I was so relieved, and the sudden realisation that everything was going to be all right caused the tears to start flowing again. And at that moment, for the very first time since my ADEs had begun, I did not feel so totally alone. Dr Brent was a prominent Consultant at the hospital, and not only had he accepted what I'd said, but he also appeared to understand my ADEs.

The following day I went back into hospital to be induced, and a few hours later I gave birth to Oliver, a healthy little boy. He was small, 6lb 1 oz, but that was to be expected as he was five weeks early. But he was strong enough to stay with me in a crib next to my bed.

The day after Oliver's birth, Dr Brent came to my ward and stood at the end of my bed. I noticed he wasn't wearing his white coat, and when he began speaking I realised he wasn't there to see me on a routine visit. He had something private he wanted to say to me, and I listened carefully as he began speaking:

*"I believe everything you have told me about your NDEs. In fact, I've had many patients who have reported having similar experiences."*

Hearing his words, my heart skipped a beat. Finally I had found someone who understood what the ADEs were, and he was a doctor, so he was bound to be able to explain why I was having them.

Dr Brent continued,

*"But I am sorry, Beverley, I am afraid my position at the hospital will not allow me to be seen to believe."*

The suddenly surge of happiness I had felt came crashing down around me. He hadn't come to tell me he would help, he was there to tell me he couldn't help because he wasn't allowed too.

*"Be strong and hold onto your faith, trust your instincts. You have a long road ahead of you, so hold on tight, and be careful about what you say and to whom you say it to."*

His words rang in my ears as he turned and walked

out of the ward, and as he disappeared the little glimmer of hope I'd felt since first telling him everything disappeared too.

Over the next few days I began to realise what Dr Brent had meant in his parting words to me. News of my ADEs had spread throughout the hospital, and I soon found myself being told I had to go and speak to a psychiatrist, then another one, and then a third psychiatrist asked to see me. It was very daunting as they all came to the maternity ward, and I was shown into a private room. Independently they questioned me relentlessly, but not one of them actually asked any direct question about the ADEs. Their questioning was rather: *When you hear a radio playing do you think it is about you?* and *Do you often feel people are talking about you?* I answered *No* to all the questions, and I was being truthful. My ADEs did not make me feel what they were suggesting at all; though granted I couldn't go in a room where a radio was playing, but only because it gave me a headache.

The last psychiatrist actually lost his temper. He stood up abruptly and said in an irate tone,

*"I've had enough, there is nothing wrong with you!"*

After I left the hospital, I never had contact with any medical professional regarding my ADEs. I just got on with my life, and when my ADEs started up again, I just resigned myself to the fact that one day I would understand them.

Then in 1991 I became pregnant with my second son, Westley-John. Once again the ADEs stopped, and I went through the entire pregnancy without having one.

However, in the autumn of 1992 I began experiencing a reality that set me on a collision course with medical professionals once again. I was pregnant a third time, only this time it was no normal pregnancy.

My husband David and I had separated, although we were both still living under the same roof. Since 1986, I had been writing a set of children's books about a group of characters called *The Snowmites*, and finally I'd secured a publishing deal with a London main stream Publishers for four hardback books. The Snowmites were also considered as a Licensing Product, and Tony Norton from a London Licensing Agency had confirmed that the estimated figure I would receive was in the region of twenty million pounds over a three-year period – UK sales alone. Everything seemed in place for The Snowmites to follow The Care Bears; my children's future and mine was now set in gold.

After David and I had separated, we both became involved in other relationships, but the woman David was involved with did not take kindly to my good fortune, and she encouraged David to seek custody of our children, as then he would be entitled to half of The Snowmites' revenue, if not more. To assist her in her gain, she telephoned Social Services and informed them I was neglecting my children. Little did she realise the enormity of her actions, and the avalanche of snow she had set rolling.

At the time, I had initially suspected I was pregnant. I was normally a slim dress size ten to twelve, with a firm and flat abdomen, but then I would notice my abdomen would suddenly look bloated. I didn't have any other pregnancy symptoms, however, so I soon dismissed the possibility of pregnancy, and put my slightly enlarged abdomen down to lack of exercise and the stress of the divorce.

One day I was home alone, and my abdomen suddenly began to grow. It happened so quickly I could hardly breathe. I was shocked when I saw it as I looked about six months pregnant, but just as suddenly as it had happened, my abdomen returned to its normal size. *What on earth has just happened?* I wondered, feeling a sense of dread; but again I put it down to stress.

It happened again and again, each time getting a little big bigger. But still it would come on suddenly and then disappear just as quickly. In the end I actually took a pregnancy test, which came out negative. I knew deep down inside it would be, as it wasn't like a normal pregnancy that has a steady growth.

Then one day I opened my door to find Tim Unston, a social worker, standing on my doorstep. He explained he wanted to speak to me about the children, and I just naturally presumed he was part of the school or nursery where my children were attending, and his visit was one of those early learning follow-up visits. I took him into the kitchen and made him a cup of coffee, and we were standing up learning against the kitchen cabinets. He was facing me, chatting away about Samantha being at school and asking about how my sons were settling in at their nursery.

Suddenly my abdomen began to enlarge. It became so big, I could actually rest my cup on the top of it. This time, I looked as if I was nine months pregnant. Ignoring what was happening, I carried on talking, but as I looked across at Tim Unston, his gaze was fixed on my abdomen, his jaw ajar - speechless from the shock, the look of fear reflected in his eyes.

Realising his horror, I tried to make light of what was happening as I didn't want him to be frightened.

*"It's all right, it happens all the time lately,"* I managed to say, not wanting to alarm him. He put down his cup and walked over to me, then he put his hand on my heart and asked,

*"Are you all right?"*

I nodded, not wanting to make a fuss. Suddenly he pulled his hand away, shook his head, then in a daze he reached in his pocket for a card.

*"Call me if you need anything,"* he said abruptly, then he rushed out of the house and slammed the door shut behind him. The moment the door closed, my abdomen returned back to its normal size.

The incident left me shaken, but I was more concerned about how it had affected Tim Unston. It was obvious by his reaction that this was something he'd never see before - so what on earth was happening to me?

On another occasion, I was making my way home after shopping in town. It was late on in the evening, so it was getting dark, and most of the shops had now closed and the streets were becoming bare. Suddenly my abdomen began to enlarge. Once again I looked about nine months pregnant, but this time my breathing changed, and I began to pant as if I actually was in labour. I could hardly walk, I struggled with each step I took, and the panic began to set in.

*I just need to get home, I'll be all right once I'm home, it will go away,* I kept thinking to myself. But then, just as I was passing the police station, my lower back suddenly locked and the pain shot through me every time I tried to take another step.

A policeman saw me and helped me into the police station. Within minutes another policeman and a policewoman were gathered around me. I was panting heavily and fast; and every time I even tried to move, the pain was horrendous, and I cried out in agony. I could hear the police officers becoming flustered.

*"Don't have it here, please don't have it here! Just hang on - you'll be at the hospital soon! Hang on, the ambulance is on its way!"* I could hear them pleading.

*"But I'm not pregnant!"* I moaned, in between panting. The pain came again and I let out an agonising scream.

The next thing I knew I was being rushed up to the hospital. I was taken straight into the delivery unit and prepared for labour.

I tried to tell the nurses I wasn't pregnant but no one

listened to me. Then a doctor came in and began to examine me to see if I was dilated enough to give birth. A cloud of concern washed over his face.

*"I don't understand,"* I heard him say, *"I can't find a baby!"*

After some more prodding and talking amongst themselves, the doctor finally told the nurses to send me down for an emergency scan. Once they had all left the delivery room to go and sort out the paperwork for the scan, my enlarged abdomen disappeared and returned to its normal slim size.

When the nurse came back into the room and saw I was slim again, she dropped the papers in her hand and rushed out to get the doctor again. He came and examined me again, and made it clear he was disturbed by my condition. Then he started telling me that he wanted to admit me into hospital so I could go for some tests; but I refused. I didn't know what was happening to me, but at that moment in time I didn't care either. I was exhausted and I just wanted to go home to be with my children.

A chill ran through me as I remembered Dr. Brent's words, *be careful about what you say and to whom you say it to.* Instinct told me not to discuss my condition anymore with the doctor or the nurses, and so I quickly gathered my belongings and signed my discharge papers - then I left the hospital and made my way home.

Shortly after this incident I had an ADE, and to say it didn't help the situation is an understatement.

## Actual Death Experience
## This Woman is Pregnant

As I fell into the first moments of the physical death, my Spirit rose up out of my physical body and I became of the Afterlife.

I only rose slightly above the physical body lying upon my bed, and noticed that my Spirit was in a similar lying position. Then I saw I was surrounded by several women in the Spirit, none of whom I'd ever met before.

The women appeared to be tending to me. Suddenly I saw Jesus step forward, and I heard him tell the women,

*"This woman is pregnant."*

Then I heard one of the women say,

*"What a beautiful way to have your confirmation!"*

Jesus then returned my Spirit back into my physical body and breathed life into me once again.

On my recovery from this ADE, I was utterly confused. It didn't make sense. *How could I be pregnant when the doctors couldn't find a baby, and when my abdomen kept changing?* Little did I know I was about to have my love for Jesus tested beyond comprehension.

Although I did not understand what was happening to me and why my body was constantly changing its natural shape – nor did I have any understanding as to why I was actually having the ADEs, the one thing I did know was that God does not lie. When Jesus spoke, He spoke only the truth. He promised my Spirit time and time again within my ADEs I'd always be protected. He proved I was. Although I was still afraid of the ADEs as they began, and the thought of having them, I knew once I was in the Spirit I had nothing to be afraid of when He was there. And He was always there.

It was inconceivable to even consider Jesus was wrong when He said I was pregnant, but at the same time I had to face reality, and I knew I was not pregnant. I felt like I'd suddenly started living a never-ending nightmare. Every night I cried myself to sleep, and my days were filled with pretending everything was all right and keeping a happy, carefree disposition. I couldn't let anyone see how I was really feeling, no one would understand. I had a new life ahead of me, a life with no financial worry, and the ability to give my children everything they needed. I was blessed with the success of The Snowmites. As far as all my friends around me were concerned, I was the luckiest woman in the world.

I can remember feeling so utterly dismayed. *Beverley if Jesus says you are pregnant then you are pregnant*, I reassured myself. *God does not lie*. But no matter how hard I tried to believe in Jesus' words, I couldn't. *Why would he do this to me? Why would Jesus tell me something that was obviously not the truth?* The moment I began

## Living With Chronic Actual Death Experiences

doubting His words - terror filled my senses, as I began to cast doubt over everything He had told me. *What if I'm not safe? What if I'm not protected in my ADEs? What will happen to me the next time I encounter an evil Spirit?*

With every ounce of faith, I held on to my belief, *my trust in Him.* I had no choice. The thought of living with ADEs and not trusting Him was simply to terrifying to bear. It wasn't just about the possibility of finding myself encountering evil Spirit. The aspect of the ADEs, I couldn't live with without Him was in the knowledge of knowing I was experiencing death. The thoughts haunted me, *how will I ever manage to come back if Jesus doesn't bring me to life again?* Indeed I had to have trust in Him.

Then in late February 1993, my abdomen again took on the shape of a nine-month pregnant woman. Only this time my children were due back, and I couldn't let them see me in that condition. So I went and asked my neighbour if she would look after my children until I could come for them and she agreed. But when she saw me she insisted on telephoning my G.P., Dr Bambus. I didn't have any choice, it was the only way she'd let me go back into my house alone. I was just grateful my children wouldn't see me in that condition, and as I sat waiting for my doctor to arrive, I kept hoping my abdomen would go back to normal.

It didn't.

When my doctor arrived, she stared at me in disbelief. I could see the look of horror in her eyes as she said,

*"I've never seen anything like this in all my twenty-seven*

*years of practice. I'll have to call for an ambulance to take you into hospital."*

I couldn't believe it! Not the hospital again, it was the last thing I needed or wanted.

*"No don't, please don't!"* I begged, *"I'm all right really, it will go away soon."*

But Dr Bambus wasn't listening. She was insistent on sending me to the hospital. In desperation, I knew I had to try and explain.

*"No, I'm all right, really. I have ADEs, and this has something to do with them. I'm not pregnant."*

My pleas fell on deaf ears, and within minutes I was back in an ambulance being rushed up to the hospital. I began panting again, and in between breaths I kept telling the ambulance men I wasn't pregnant, explaining that I just kept swelling up.

This time I was rushed into A&E, and wheeled off into a side room. My breathing had become erratic and I couldn't catch my breath. I could hear the nurses frantically saying,

*"Breathe, breathe, breathe for me sweetheart!"*

But I couldn't. Then everything started going black as I suddenly began to fall into unconsciousness. I sensed the separation, as the ADE began.

## Actual Death Experience
### The Birth of the Child in the Spirit

As I fell into the first moments of the physical death, my Spirit rose up out of my physical body and I became of the Afterlife.

I only rose a few inches above my physical body lying upon the hospital bed, and I noticed that my Spirit was also in a lying position. I could hear one of the nurses shouting, *'We're losing her!'*, and I could see them bustling around my physical body.

Suddenly, a vivid white light appeared and lit up the entire room. Everywhere fell into a sudden peacefulness, and the figures around me began fading away. The presence of the white light seemed to drown out the noise in the room, and everything suddenly seemed distant.

The white light had a strange, beautiful aura; it seemed to vibrate intensely and then soften. It was majestic. Never before had I ever seen such a beautiful light.

Suddenly the Spirit of Trevor Enstone appeared on my right hand side, and I heard him say: *'When I say push I want you to push.'*

The white light seemed to engulf the entire room, and at that moment I heard the most beautiful sound, and I knew it was the presence of Angels within the light. Then I heard his Spirit say, *'Push!'* and I felt myself push as hard as I could.

At that very moment, a new-born baby rose up from out of my Spirit. The Child in the Spirit was born by rising upwards out of my abdomen. I could see the baby was surrounded by a beautiful glowing light, and the presence of the Angels became so intense, it seemed as if they were singing to the baby.

Suddenly the baby then became caught up within the alluring light in the room, and as it absorbed the Child in the Spirit, the light became small, and as it started to disappear I saw Trevor Enstone's Spirit rush upwards to chase after the light.

Jesus then returned my Spirit back into my physical body and breathed life into me once again.

As I regained consciousness, I opened my eyes and saw two nurses to my right hand side and a nurse standing on my left hand side. One of the nurses to my right had a needle in her hand, and suddenly I felt an intense sharp pain in the top of my right leg as she injected me with the needle. Then the nurse on my left did the same, and I felt the intense pain again at the top of my left leg.

The darkness came quickly as I began to fall into unconsciousness again, but this time it was drug-induced. As my eyelids fluttered and I tried to fight the drugs, I felt myself smile and a warm sense of relief flowed through me. My love for Jesus had been saved. God did not lie. I had been pregnant after all.

## *Frustration Of My Heart*

*The thunder has broken
With the falling rains
The sky clouds of great mist
I stood and saw the brightness
In the lightning flashes that struck
Before the storm*

*The greyness lingers
In the breath of the heavens
And to weak the wind
To blow the clouds away*

*I be of awaiting
For the winds so strong
To bring the summer
From this winter of sun again*

# 9

## Living With Chronic Actual Death Experiences

### Part Two

I have two memories over a four day period following the administration of the drugs at the hospital's A&E department. The first memory I can recall is being stood up in the middle of a room. I was so heavily drugged that I was not able to support myself; two people, one on my left and the other on my right, stood next to me holding me up. I could just see the shadowy figures of others in the room, and I could hear myself beginning to speak to them. I noticed my words sounded slurred and I was apologising to them for not being able to speak properly - then the blackness came again, and I lost consciousness while still standing.

The second memory I have was waking up in a bed within a private room, and Tim Unston was sat on the end of the bed. Then the blackness came again and I lost consciousness.

I was admitted into the hospital on the Friday evening, and apart from the two memories mentioned, I had no recollection of the events that took place over the entire weekend. But my medical records to which I was allowed access in 1997 stated that I was actually up on my feet and walking around, and although I was apparently talking about my ADEs, I made no mention of encountering Jesus within the Afterlife.

When I regained full conscious awareness, I was somewhat surprised and a little confused. *Why was I still at the hospital?* "*What did the nurses do to me?*" I asked a nurse who came into my room, but she just smiled reassuringly and told me I would be seeing the Consultant later that afternoon, and he would explain everything.

When I finally sat down in front of Dr D'Sims, I had no idea he was a Psychiatrist, or the fact that I had been sectioned under the mental health act. I thought he was just a normal doctor.

The consultation was brief but I didn't need long to realise something was wrong, very wrong indeed. Dr D'Sims was asking the same strange questions to which I had been subjected when I had given birth to my son Oliver.

"*When you hear a radio playing, do you think it is about you? Do you think other people are talking about you?*" His questions were disturbing but I still didn't understand the full extent of what was going on around me. I answered his questions truthfully and I could sense he was getting annoyed with me. Eventually Dr D'Simms told me he'd see me again the following day, and I was sent back to my room.

I was worried about my children, I told a nurse I

wanted to go home and asked to sign myself out as I didn't need to see the doctor again. The nurse frowned and explained that I couldn't discharge myself as I was being detained, and that is how I actually found out I had been sectioned. Dr D'Simms had not told me he was a Psychiatrist or the fact that I was being detained.

On the following day, before my scheduled consultation with Dr D'Simms, a nurse came into my room and told me I could go home: I was free to leave. It was all very bewildering, but I didn't stop to ask any questions, I gathered my things together and called a taxi to take me home.

When I arrived home, I was greeted with hostility from my husband David. Within a matter of minutes the situation turned into a violent argument, resulting in my head being pushed through the glass pane of the kitchen door. That was the turning point for me. I knew I could no longer live in the same house as David. I had to take decisive action to protect myself, and so I decided it was time to seek the advice of a lawyer.

The following morning I met with a local solicitor, and as soon as she heard my account of the previous evening, she decided to make an application to the court for an injunction.

Three hours later, I was sitting in front of a Judge repeating the events that had taken place after I had returned home. The Judge ordered the injunction. By order of the court, David had to leave the matrimonial home, and if he refused, the police could remove him.

When David learned of his fate, he wasn't happy but he accepted the decision of the court and left the house.

The past few days had certainly been traumatic for me, but finally I was able just to be with my children and relax. I needed to clear my head to think about the future and make some decisions about what the children and I were going to do. There was no turning back now, the events of the previous evening had sealed the fate of my marriage - David and I had finally started on the path of divorce.

The following day, I got a telephone call from my solicitor. She wanted to see me urgently, as David had retained his own solicitor and there was to be another court hearing later that day. It seemed a bizarre course of action and my solicitor didn't know the reason for the hearing, but nevertheless I had to attend. I dressed quickly, and after I had arranged for my neighbour to look after the children, I left the house. On my way out I picked up the morning's post and put the letters in my bag - not giving them a second thought, as I made my way to my solicitor's office.

By lunchtime, we were sat in a courtroom in front of another Judge. Finally my solicitor was able to explain what was going on - David's solicitor had made an application to the court for an injunction against me! It was ludicrous! Why would anyone held bound over by an injunction then apply for an injunction themselves? It was mindboggling and the Judge himself did not seem impressed, but he had no choice, he had to hear the evidence supporting David's application.

As I sat listening to David's solicitor's case, I went numb with shock. Their case was based on my recent admission into hospital for my ADEs. And then they delivered a startling blow: Dr D'Simms had apparently told them that he wanted me back in the hospital. No one thought to question the merit of the revelation: for how could a Doctor even speak to a Solicitor about my health without my permission? It was not allowed, and if he had done such then he had committed professional misconduct. Did he do it, or were David's solicitors just playing the legal system in an abuse of justice?

The Judge had no choice. On hearing the evidence, he had to make an order, and then he listed the case to be heard again in ten days' time. I sat in total disbelief as I listened to the Judge's decision. He ordered that I was to return to the hospital for a second assessment, and David could return to our home to be with our children. The decision had been made, and this court order ruling was set to turn my whole world upside down, and set me down a path that would see all the professionals involved in my life back in court some three years later.

I had to go to the hospital straight from the court, but when I arrived there Dr D'Simms wasn't on duty. A few hours later he turned up, and when he saw me he seemed surprised.

In a bewildered tone he asked me, *"What are you doing here, Beverley? Do you like it here or have you come to see me?"*

I couldn't believe what I was hearing. I was there only because he had told the court that he wanted me back in hospital, but when I told him such, his attitude suddenly changed and he became flustered.

"*I did not say anything of the sort, young lady. I don't want you here. You don't belong in hospital. Go home, I'm not allowing you to stay here!*"

My thoughts whirled with shock. *Why had David's solicitors made up such a terrible lie and purposely submitted it as evidence in a court of law? What was going on?*

Dr D'Simms opened the door to the ward. He stared at me intensely. "*Go home,*" he repeated as he closed the ward door, and left me standing alone in the waiting area. As I stood there trying to take in everything that had happened, it suddenly dawned on me: I can't go home, David is there! I can't go back to the house. If I can't stay at the hospital then where am I going to go? I don't have anything, no money, no clothes – nothing. *What am I going to do now?*

Dr D'Simms had refused to allow me back into the hospital, and I couldn't go back to my house. I couldn't even speak to my solicitor as it was now past office hours.

And that is how it happened - I had suddenly become homeless. My babies had been ripped out of my arms, and I had nothing. Everything I owned except for the clothes on my back was back at the house.

I stumbled out of the hospital, the tears streaming down my face. *What am I going to do? Where can I go now?*

I was dazed and in a state of shock. I had nowhere

to go, no nearby family. I was out on the streets, lost and alone and so very, very heartbroken. How on earth has all this happened to me? I hadn't done anything wrong. I had ADEs, not a mental illness, but even that thought brought a harrowing realisation, *What if I had been sick? What if I had needed treatment? Is this how the professionals treat people who they think is ill?*

Hungry and cold, I walked the streets for hours until finally I found shelter in an old workman's wooden hut on a building site. As I sat huddled in a dark, dusty corner, the anxiety hit hard. I wanted to be at home with my babies - safe and warm, making sure they were all right. Being there if they woke up in the middle of the night to comfort them back to sleep. But I couldn't. My right to my motherhood had been stolen - destroyed by lies. But who had lied? Was it David's solicitors or was it Dr D'Simms?

I reached into my bag and pulled out the letters that had arrived in the morning's post. They were just bills, all except for one. Tearing open the envelope, I saw it was a letter from the hospital. My eyes scanned the words:

*Dear Ms Gilmour, We write in reference to your recent admission into hospital after attending the A&E department. We wish to offer you our sincere apology, as the section you were detained under was an illegal sectioning, and you should never have been detained. We do hope this has not caused you any inconvenience or distress.*

It was a letter of apology from the hospital informing me that I had been illegally sectioned. It is not an acceptable practice to access a patient for a mental health illness when they are under the influence of drugs, and I had been given the drugs before I was assessed.

The hospital staff had separated me from my children, and then they wrote hoping their action had not caused me any distress! The fierce pain I felt in my heart crushed me, and at that very moment I felt it breaking into a thousand tiny pieces, and the pain in my head was unbearable. My head felt on fire; and then suddenly it exploded, sending a wave of heat escalating over my entire head. The shock of losing my children and being made homeless was of such an incredible force, I could barely breathe.

Little did I realise, as I sat there huddled in pain, that the intense heat inside my head was caused by my higher consciousness, my Spiritual mind being opened abruptly. The horrendous shock to my consciousness had triggered a change in my perception, and so began a whole new phase within my ADEs.

Over the next six months I sat in courtroom after courtroom, listening solemnly as my motherhood was put on trial because of my ADEs. Although the medical professionals were now no longer suggesting I was suffering from a mental illness, David's solicitors were insinuating that I was, and they were accusing the medical professionals of misconduct. They even submitted an affidavit claiming Dr D'Simms had committed perjury. It was supposed to have been just a normal custody hearing, but David's solicitors had turned it into a malice witch hunt.

Finally the High Courts of London ruled that I was

sane and perfectly capable of looking after my children, regardless of my ADEs. At last I was reunited with them, but I had indeed been scarred by the whole traumatic experience. I no longer trusted anyone: not doctors, not social workers, not anyone. I refused point blank to speak to anyone about my ADEs. I wouldn't even go to my local G.P practice to tell them about the fiery pain in my head that I was constantly experiencing. I just forced myself to get on with my life.

Although I had been awarded the care of my children, we never got anything else. We didn't get our home back or any of our personal belongings. David got to keep everything, and he resided in our four-bedroom family home with his new partner. He kept everything that belonged to our children, their beds, blankets, clothes and even their toys, and I never saw any of my clothes or personal paperwork again either.

My children and I had to move into a one-bedroom part furnished apartment. It was in a rough area: my neighbours were alcoholics and drug users, and there was a constant police presence in the street. We had a cooker but no pots and pans or plates. We had an old worn sofa but no television, and we had to sleep together in a double bed that had most definitely seen better days - huddled together, keeping each other warm. Week by week I bought a new plate or a candle. I was forced to claim state benefits, as David refused to pay child support. It was a hard life, but regardless of what little we did have, we had each other, and we had love.

I did become a very over-protective mother. If the children ever needed to see a doctor, or any health-care professional - even any one to one session they had to have with their teachers, I stood by them watching intently, and insisting on reading everything anyone wrote down about them.  I became hated by the professionals, but I didn't care.  I wasn't going to let anyone put down on paper anything that wasn't true.

I was caught up in a reality that was splitting me in two. Within my ADEs, Jesus was showing me He wanted me to reveal His teachings.  But I couldn't.  I was too afraid of what the professionals would do to me and my children. The only sector I felt secure enough to confide in was the Church, and so began my search for a priest who would help me.

Although every priest or minister I spoke to said they believed me and they would help me (except for the priest I mentioned in chapter four), not one of them did anything about my revelation of being with Christ in the Spirit - in having the ADEs.  I became worn down, exhausted by the constant contradictions. How could the Church accept my truth of being with Jesus in ADEs, and yet do nothing about it? The reality was ludicrous.

My ADEs started occurring more frequently.  I was now having them three to four times a month. Sometimes, I'd even have two in one week. They would only happen whenever my children were not around me.

I was now no longer able to have a natural sleep, but I did notice a change that had never happened before: I was absorbing my children's energy during the day. I couldn't get out of my bed in the mornings until after they had got up. I knew they needed me to look after them, and the mother in me was determined to overcome the pain I was feeling: the stiffness in my limbs and the constant burning pain in my head.

I could feel them, their presence around me, as much as my children needed me to look after them - I knew they were saving my life. Without them, I would have given up. So many times, I wanted to just let go and succumb to the physical death I was experiencing. Let go and not come back to the pain and weariness. But whenever I had such thoughts, I would find myself fighting back: *No, no, I can't do that to my children! I can't leave them. I can't let them wake up and find me dead in my bed!*

It wasn't just my children's energy I was absorbing. After being reunited with them, I re-connected with a dear friend, Kym Warham. Her beauty was incredible, her heart sincere. Her physical appearance was truly stunning, her physique toned and well looked after. She was dedicated to keeping in shape, and she had an enormous amount of energy; so much so that she had to do an eighty minute workout exercise programme every morning just to feel balanced.

I began absorbing Kym's energy, and at the same time, I noticed I was absorbing her knowledge. I began to look after my own physical body - exercising and trying to eat well. Kym would often visit me after her workout class. She would arrive feeling totally refreshed, but within ten minutes of sharing my company, she'd be drained, and she'd laugh at how she could do an eighty minute strenuous workout and feel fine, but after being with me for a few minutes, she felt she needed to go to bed. She was a beautiful person, and little did she know her willingness to allow me to absorb her energy was giving me back my womanhood, giving me back that part of my life.

The change in my perception brought about another ability that was startling. I was now able to sense Spirit around me, wherever I went. The room temperature would suddenly drop, and I'd pick up on the movement by tracing the vibes. I began to sense a very high-pitched constant communication at the front of my right brain, and when Jesus wanted me to take notice of something going on around me, I would get a very loud ringing (similar to when you have a hearing test) in the left side of my brain. Then I would go totally deaf in both ears, and as the ringing stopped, I'd become aware of what people were saying or simply doing around me. This would last only seconds, and as soon as I'd taken in what Jesus wanted me to see or hear, He'd return my normal hearing.

Over the following three years I struggled every day. Not a day went by when I didn't feel the horrendous pain in my head and limbs. I gritted my teeth to hide the pain I was experiencing, and smiled to hide the sadness. I was going against Jesus and I knew it, but I couldn't fight the fear for what the professionals had done to me. Jesus guided me to reveal all but I remained silent.

In the end the sadness became too over-bearing. I knew His teachings were for us all - to teach us how to become better people, to mend the ever increasing broken society we were living in. But apart from the Churches, I could not speak of His name to anyone.

It was 1993 when the Spiritual writings began - the Who Am I? Prophesies of Jesus. In not being able to speak His name, my higher consciousness, the Spiritual mind, would force me into a trance state of consciousness, and I would write page after page of Spiritual writings, revealing His name and His teachings within my ADEs. The explanation for every single ADE became written down. Every night for three years once my children were safely in bed, I'd find myself writing these pages.

I began to understand the importance of His teachings and how they would change mankind for the better - our evolution. In this trance state of consciousness, I would come to illustrate the working of the human mind, and show how the three levels of consciousness interacted with each other in the relationship between the physical mind and the Spiritual mind - the cause of mental illness and the coma - the understanding of addictive behaviour. The knowledge was empowering, and I knew I was wrong to remain silent. I had to let people know about Jesus and His teachings. But how could I? How could I ever trust another professional person again?

Finally I found a way. I would write it down in a letter - that way I could tell the reader of my ADEs, and explain that when I had them I encountered Jesus to bring back His teachings.

I wrote to the Prime Minister, Her Royal Highness Queen Elizabeth II, the Pope and the Archbishop of Canterbury. I informed these recipients of the court hearings, of how the professionals had abused the British Justice system, and asked for a public inquiry - knowing then that everyone would finally be able to understand my ADEs, and acknowledge they were not part of a mental illness just as the High Courts of London had done. It made logical sense to me that these were the right people to be told about the Visitation of Christ.

In His *Who Am I?* Prophesies, Jesus had given a promise that the Monarchy would be restored to its former glory, and the importance for a Government rule to work with the people, and in return to be respected by the people. How the untruth to the system was as a cancer to the body.

The only reply I got was from the Archbishop of Canterbury, thanking me for my letter and acknowledging the contents. Once again the Church had accepted my truth but this time at a much higher level. I waited in anticipation believing that something as important as Jesus' visitation was worthy of a public inquiry. The public inquiry never came.

I waited and waited - day in, day out. But still no one did anything to help me. I couldn't understand people. What was wrong with them? Did they truly not consider Jesus as being important? Were His new Spiritual teachings of so little interest? Did abuse of the British legal system not deem an investigation? Was a mother's life worth so little? Was the separation of children from their mother and the destruction of their home considered of so little worth, of no concern? What kind of people had we become not to care about Justice or the value of life?

The emotion of anger raged within my heart, and

the more intense my emotions became the more intense the fiery pain in my head burned. I couldn't live this way any longer. I had to do something about it. But what? What could I do about it?

It was now 1996, and some people may think it was always going to happen the way it did. The *Who Am I? Prophesies of Jesus*, and the letters had first to be written to set up the next chain of events. I suspect these people may be right if they do think such, for the Higher Consciousness, the Spiritual mind, can tune into the future. Many times, I penned events that later came true.

I did notice that during those three years, 1993 to 1996, I often felt I was walking ten steps behind myself. I would ask myself a question such as, *Why am I doing this now?* and I would sense I knew the answer but it felt as if the answer was up on a shelf that I couldn't reach, and so I'd have to search harder within myself for the answer. The Higher Consciousness is a level of consciousness that protects the individual's life and love. Therefore the events that began to unfold in 1996 were obviously unavoidable. I was angry and I wanted justice.

The existence of these Spiritual writings allowed me to walk into the local County Court offices. I was going to sue the people who had hurt my children and destroyed my life. I issued three writs: one against the Area Health Authority, the second against Social Services, and the third against Trevor Enstone - the man who had been involved within my ADEs. He was now in prison, convicted of being a Paedophile, and so the writ against him had to be sent care of the Prison service. The reason for this last writ was founded upon the fact that in 1993 when he and I had been friends - he betrayed me, and although he pretended to still be my friend at the time, I later discovered he was actually assisting David's solicitors in the custody case, and he had also assualted me both in 1992 and 1993.

I worded each of the writs carefully, under the heading *Man has been within the Visitation of Christ*. Then I wrote the affidavits with precise detail:

*'I have Actual Death Experiences and Man is within the Visitation of Christ - this is my belief. If this belief is deemed to be false, then I am suffering from a mental illness, and if I am of such suffering, then I claim the medical professionals caused such by separating me from my children and making me homeless. I therefore claim damages for the sum of twenty million pounds. The amount I lost when I lost my career and my motherhood.'*

The case against the Area Health Authority was sealed when I included within the affidavit the letter of apology I had received from them in 1993.

There was also another more serious realisation that held the Area Health Authority responsible, which I didn't know about until I got a copy of all my medical records. Dr D'Simms had signed the authorisation for the sectioning but next to his signature he had crossed out two dates. He had obviously added his signature days after the actual section took place. This was proved for on an staff attendance sheet Dr D'Simms wasn't on duty on the day of my admission or the day after. He wasn't even listed as being one of the emergency call out consultants for that weekend. So he couldn't have been present during my admission into the hospital. He had falsified my medical records.

Social Services, however, decided to put forward a Stone Wall Defence, which meant they were denying all allegations. I watched as the court proceedings continued. The Area Health Authority, concerned that they would be fully liable, decided to send me a copy of my records held by Social Services as they had requested disclosure. The records showed that Social Services had dismissed Tim Unston , the Social Worker, for professional misconduct. He had also falsified my medical records. It seemed Social Services were once again trying to abuse the British Justice system, playing games with the court with their Stone Wall Defence, and so I made an application to the Court to join the two writs together. The Judge agreed.

The one case was now against both Area Health Authority and the Social Services. As the case proceeded, I simply sat back and watched as both sets of professionals blamed each other for the professional misconduct.

Twelve months later, I decided to apply to the court to have the third case against Trevor Enstone joined to the proceedings. It was time the professionals understood the error of their ways, and to stop playing games with the legal system. Fearing the bad publicity, as the court was prepared to grant my application, Area Health Authority and Social Services decided to settle out of court. The money I was awarded was not of my concern; I agreed to the settlement on condition that both sets of professionals acknowledge that I had never suffered from any form of mental health illness, and that my ADEs, although unexplained, were real. They agreed. My ADEs had finally been acknowledged.

Now the Area Health Authority and Social Services had sanctioned my ADEs, I felt justice conerning them had been granted but the whole truth had still not been completely told. The professional's actions had made me bankrupt - even though I was on Income Support at the time. When Mr Enstone's lawyers found out about my bankruptcy status - they used it to dismiss my case against their client, and although over the years I have indeed tried to get him to tell the truth and admit what he did to me - my attempts have all been in vain as he still refuses to speak the truth, and give me the peace of mind I have always yearned for.

It is fair to say that the court cases did help me in other ways. Although I did not get to give any evidence verbally, the fact that I encountered Jesus within my ADEs was now in the mindset of the medical professionals, and I was finally able to find a new G.P who realised it was important to listen without being judgemental.

The professionalism of my new G.P Dr. Curzon was outstanding, and he was the first doctor to start treating me for chronic ADEs. The first request he issued was for me to have brain scans to ensure it was not a tumour that was causing the ADEs. And then he requested other tests, but all the test results came back clear. Over time, Dr Curzon restored my trust in medical professionals, and eventually I was able to tell him that when I had an ADE, I met with Jesus. I stayed with Dr Curzon right up to when he retired, and even then he tried to find someone suitable to replace him in looking after me.

Eventually, I found Dr Jenny Franklin. She also proved to be an outstanding doctor. She knew the difficulties I faced - the medical sector didn't understand ADEs enough but she treated me to the best of her ability, and it did make my life more comfortable and easier to bear. The burning pain in my head was so intense - sometimes I couldn't even touch my head let alone brush my hair. Some days I would find myself sitting on the sofa, unable to move.

Being with Jesus in the ADEs proved to be an extreme emotional journey in my physical life. I couldn't enjoy the normal aspects of life as a woman. Although, I longed to find love with a man in a normal healthy physical relationship, I couldn't. Everyone who came into my life, appeared to have encountered me for their own Spiritual growth, both men and women. I would find myself absorbing their energy and then I would reflect back their suppressed emotions to them. Most everyone who I met would complain of having severe headaches and feeling exhausted whenever they were in my company. Sometimes, I would just have to touch a person, and the energy would flow through our bodies. Other times I would simply need to talk to a person over the telephone to absorb their energy. The energy was so powerful - everyone I connected with could feel it.

I know Jesus didn't instruct me to take on the Court Cases but I don't regret my actions. I may have been wrong in doing what I did, as my desire was fuelled by an anger, a negative emotion. But when all is said and done, the court cases were the only way forward for me, a stepping stone to eventually finding my courage to speak out about Jesus and His sacred *Who Am I? Spiritual Teachings* in His journey of my Spirit.

I love Jesus with all my heart. I could never deny Him, but first the Mother in me had to protect her children: the innocence of life itself.

## The Fairy Tale

### *I Am What I Am*

*I was as a Lamb in slaughter*
*And they preyed upon my Soul*
*They brought me down*
*And I became crippled*
*They threw stones at me*
*And I became bruised*
*But they did not know*
*I was with Christ in the Spirit*

*After their feast, Our Lord picked me up*
*And I stood stronger in His love*
*Than I had ever stood before*
*Now if they come in War*
*I am prepared for Battle*
*But if they come in Peace*
*I am prepared to share with them*
*My thoughts.*

# 10

## The Fairy Tale

I was about six years old, that day I was out playing with my three cousins. We had just been to visit our Grandmother earlier, and although it was still only mid-afternoon, we had already got ourselves into all sorts of mischief that day.

We were outside playing, walking around the neighbourhood: knocking on doors and then running away, taunting those who tried to catch us but hadn't been quick enough, and throwing mud heaps at the passing cars then ducking behind the bushes in a fit of giggles.

Eventually we found ourselves wandering around the quaint little village of Claughton in Oxton. It was only about half a mile away from our own houses: the stoned pavements and tarmac surfaces of Glover Street and Kingsland Road with the terraced houses hugged together in rows. But the difference in the scenery around the tiny village with the detached houses, neatly trimmed lawns and expertly pruned gardens, made it seem like we lived a million miles away in a different part of the world.

I had never been a delicate little girl who was always wearing pretty dresses with silky ribbons in my hair. I was the classic tomboy in every sense. I would

## The Fairy Tale

always have scuffed knees and a mucky face. My mousey brown hair was cut so short and uneven that many people thought I actually was a boy!

I was always climbing trees or racing against my cousins on our home-made go-karts made up from bits of wood, pieces of string, and the discarded wheels of broken prams. We would often go exploring old, derelict houses, finding useless discarded items, which we would then pretend were lost treasures, and we would pile up our rusty bounty on our go-karts and take it to our secret den up at Arnie Hill to divide it out equally amongst ourselves.

The big old house on the hill in the village was huge and set far back off the lane. The front garden looked almost as big as a football field, and it was surrounded by an old historic castle stone wall; you could just see the tips of at least a dozen apple trees dotted around the garden.

The temptation to sneak into the garden and steal a few apples was just too good to resist. Finding a gap in the wall behind a hedge of bushes, we all squeezed our way through it into the garden, and I was soon sitting on a branch half-way up one of the trees, plucking the apples and throwing them down to my eagerly waiting cousins.

Suddenly, I heard shouting! When I looked up across the vast private gardens, I saw a man running towards us. He had his clenched hand held up in the air and he was waving it around. He looked very angry.

Even before I had managed to get down out of the apple tree, my three cousins had scampered, fleeing like frightened little rabbits. I scurried back through the hole in the wall - only to see the distant figures of my three cousins running away. I knew I would never be able to catch up with them. Hearing the huge iron gates opening behind me, I froze, and sheer panic swept through me. I didn't want the angry man to catch me, but what could I do? I thought about crouching behind the bushes, but I knew he would most probably look there. I had to find somewhere to hide and I had to find it quickly before he came out of the gates.

The only other building nearby was a Church opposite the house. I ran across the grass lawns and pulled open the big heavy doors of the Church and darted inside. It was deserted - not a soul in sight. In my haste I swiftly slipped underneath one of the wooden pews and curled up into a tiny ball. My heart pounded loudly as I listened out for the Church doors to open. I was convinced the angry man was about to rush in and drag me out from my hiding place. I knew I would be in terrible trouble if he found me.

I don't know how long I stayed curled up underneath the pew, hidden and feeling scared, but after a while I finally crept out from my hiding place and stood for a moment, wondering what I should do next.

I could not remember ever being inside a Church before. It was a huge old building and it looked amazing. I was captivated by the magnificent view as I stood in awe of the surrounding beauty. I sensed something about my surroundings that intrigued me. It was a setting of calmness in the still silence.

## The Fairy Tale

I began to walk slowly down the side aisle nearest to the wall. There were several enormous stained glass windows showing different pictures of people, and I noticed all the people seemed to look very sad. The sun-rays shone down in through the windows, reflecting the most incredible shades of colours I had ever seen, and in between the flickering colours I could see tiny pockets of dust floating around in the air. The wooden pews and surrounding wood glimmered with a silvery shine and I caught the whiff of a mixed odour: the smell of wood polish blending with a strong scent of heavy muskiness.

Mesmerized by my surroundings I continued to walk down the aisle; then as I stood gazing up at one particular stained glass window, I leaned against a wooden pew. The wood creaked, echoing loudly around the empty Church.

I jumped forward, frightened by the sudden intrusive crackling noises. Everywhere I looked, I could see lots of wooden doors leading off to other places. I stood in anticipation, staring separately at each of the doors and waited for that familiar sense of dread to swallow me up. But nothing happened, and I realised I wasn't afraid of these doors; not like those at my cousin's house, where all the doors terrified me; especially the dining-room door, which led into the garage.

I would stand rigid just staring at that door, not even daring to walk past it because I was afraid, afraid it would suddenly open and my mother's brother would be standing there, waiting to take me away to play his secret little game. I didn't understand why I was afraid of him, I just knew I didn't like him. But here in this big, beautiful building with all the doors, and even with the many darkened corners, I wasn't scared. I felt safe.

There upon the walls surrounding the central altar, I saw several pictures of a man, and on the back wall there was a huge stained glass window with a picture of the same man standing next to a woman. But in the paintings I could see that he had blood gushing down from his head.

*Why was this man bleeding? He looked hurt. What was happening to him? Why wasn't anyone helping him?*

I didn't understand his story and I felt a sense of sadness for him.

I began exploring the Church and I soon came across a big colourful picture book - it was a children's bible. I flipped through the pages and then I saw Him again, but this time He was sitting with a group of children. I just knew He was a good man. There was something about that picture that told me He was a man who loved children. Whoever he was, I just knew He was a man who would never hurt a child, and suddenly a love inside my heart for Him - just ignited.

The day I ran into that Church was the start of my relationship with Jesus. After that day, I would sneak into that Church whenever I could, rather than play outside with my cousins. It was usually empty, but when it wasn't, I would simply hide away until I was sure everyone had left. Sometimes the vicar would still be in there tidying up, and I would hide behind the long velvet curtains waiting for him to leave.

## The Fairy Tale

On one occasion, I even found myself locked inside the Church, but I didn't become scared, I just searched for a way out. Eventually, I found a door which lead down to the basement, and then I found a broken window which didn't close properly. The broken window then became my secret entrance. I would just sit in the Church lost in a world of a child's innocent imagination.

In the children's bible, I had read He was a King, and soon He became a very special King to me. I would pretend I was a Princess and He was my King and the Church was our castle. I would sit for hours at the high Altar pretending I had a very special garden, and He would come to my kingdom looking for a Princess. The sun's beams shone down on me as I sat alone playing my game, illuminating the Church and creating an even more magical ambience for my very own Fairy Tale.

In my innocence I created a love, and in my love for Jesus, I had brought alive a King who came and rescued me from the dragon before chasing the shadows away.

In the *Who am I?* journey of my Spirit, Jesus first brought me His teachings of the Fairy Tale in the September of 1992. Within my ADEs Jesus told me a story about The Tree of the Gold Keys. It was a beautiful Fairy Tale about a Princess who had a very special garden filled with the finest White Roses, and every day she sat in her garden waiting for her handsome Prince to arrive. However, in 1992 I had no understanding for His teaching. At the time I made no connection to my childhood.

However, it wasn't long after His teaching of the

Fairy Tale that Jesus took my Spirit to meet with the Spirit of the late Walt Disney for the first time. When I recovered from this ADE, I wrongly presumed Jesus must have given me the Fairy Tale to give to Walt's Spirit, when in fact the truth of the matter was that my Spirit offered Walt's Spirit my Fairy Tale, and in exchange I wanted Walt to teach me how to weave his magic and become a great storyteller.

It is not surprising, therefore, that Walt's Spirit was, to say the least, somewhat amused on our first encounter.

Actual Death Experience
**Teach Me Your Magic**

In the Spirit I rose up out of my physical body and became of the Afterlife. I hovered in mid-air, and beneath me I could see my lifeless physical body lying upon my bed. Then I felt myself drifting along as I moved towards the bedroom window.

I passed through the bedroom window - out into the openness. I held myself suspended in midair, then suddenly I felt myself flying through the starlit sky at great speed. I flew upwards, past the drifting clouds, and I heard myself call out the name of Jesus. The wind brushed against my face as I flew through the air.

A familiar sense of calmness engulfed my entire senses, and I felt the presence of Christ to my left-hand side. Suddenly a huge bright glowing white light was upon me. In a moment's rush the heavens lit up intensely and I felt myself being absorbed into the white light.

## The Fairy Tale

I felt myself being gently guided downwards. Then I found myself walking down the corridor within a large building.

The surface of the wooden floor shone with a glimmering light, and along the walls the glass in the wood-framed windows sparkled brightly. It was breathtaking. I could feel the essence of creativity in every brick.

A moment later I reached a door to a room, and there I saw two strong-looking men standing outside each side of the door. I knew the two men were there for security, as you could not go into this room unless you had been invited. When the two men saw me they instantly moved away from the door to allow me to enter.

There inside the room I saw the Spirit of the late Walt Disney. He was standing beside a desk, and I knew he had been expecting me. Then I suddenly heard myself saying to him,

*"I want you to teach me the magic of being a Storyteller, and in exchange I will share with you the Fairy Tale Jesus has given me."*

Walt smiled and seemed to be pondering upon my words. Then he replied,

*"I admire your cheek!"* He stepped backwards, and with a wave of his hand a three-foot animated Mickey Mouse appeared, followed by a three-foot animated Donald Duck. The two characters began chasing each other around the room, and I heard Walt laugh, and then

he spoke the words, *"Shall we get started then?"*

Jesus then returned my Spirit back into my physical body and breathed life into me once again.

In the years that followed, Jesus took my Spirit within my Actual Death Experiences on many occasions to meet again with the Spirit of Walt Disney. In many ways I became his apprentice, his novice, and as he took me under his wing the Snowmite storylines took on a whole new lease of life.

I first began writing the Snowmites in 1986 when I was on maternity leave with my daughter Samantha, and when my ADEs began in 1987, I soon noticed that I was using them to draw inspiration, but my creative writing still lacked one of the fundamental rules - depth of character.

To say Walt worked me hard is an understatement. Everything he taught me oozed with magic. But incredibly, it wasn't just an endless flight of fantasy; everything he taught me had an element of common sense: *"It's not believable if people can't relate to your story. Put yourself in the story. Become the story. Become the characters"*. And that is exactly what I did.

Within my ADEs, I became my character *Zandeer, the Beautiful Spirit of Children,* and I went in search of the *Mysterious Crystal of Life.*

When I began writing down the *Who Am I? Prophecies of Jesus,* and the many letters of Spiritual Writings, I also found myself writing about a whole new

## The Fairy Tale

fantasy world involving the Snowmites and their character origins in the creation of *The Spirit Council*. The Spirit Council were known as The Spirits of Love and they inhabited a magical mysterious world called *Heavenina*. Their charge was to protect the Mysterious Crystal of Life from *Perilon*, who plotted to steal it and absorb its powers for himself - granting him the ability to open the *Pathway of Time between Heavenina and Earth*.

The Spirit Council had to leave Heavenina to journey the heavens in a bid to protect the Mysterious Crystal of Life. But Perilon created a fierce storm, commanding a bolt of lightning to strike the Spirit Council in a bid to destroy them. The bolt of lightning missed the Spirit Council and hit the Mysterious Crystal of Life, separating it into seven independent Crystals, and all but one zoomed off at a tremendous speed into the Universe.

Nymous, the Spirit Lord, ordered the Spirit Council to go in search of the missing pieces of the Mysterious Crystal of Life, and charged them to remain with the Crystal they found until they encountered a true Guardian who would stay with the missing pieces of the Crystal and protect it from Perilon.

Zandeer is the first Spirit of Love to find one of the missing Crystals. She discovers it upon a deserted iceberg on the planet Earth. Transforming the iceberg into an enchanting *Island of Ice*, Zandeer then creates the Snowmites to live with her while she waits for the true Guardian to arrive. Then she will be able to return to her home in the heavens.

The words just poured out onto the paper. But it

wasn't just the Snowmite Books that took on a whole new meaning.

Walt's art was in the moving image, and so the Snowmites ventured into the animated short, and then the feature film script *Snowmite Magic*, which birthed an even greater expansion, creating an innovative structure – taking the film and publishing industry to a new dimension of storytelling with nine more animated feature film scripts. Combine the features with the animated shorts, and together with Walt, I had created an incredible never-ending magical story with 258 new elite characters.

And then came his new Theme Park, in which his favourite ride was the roller-coaster. I explored his paradise with fascination and an eagerness of the visionary. And in my physical life, I brought his magic back to share with the world.

Within my Actual Death Experiences, Jesus was showing me the most incredible sights. I saw buildings made from precious gems, water holes enriched with crystals, and the most exquisite of gardens. The majestic beauty inspired my senses, and its mystical reality danced within my conscious thoughts, and the Snowmites' world began to mirror the heavenly paradise I'd come to witness in my ADEs.

In 1991, even before Walt's input, I had signed with a Literary Agent and secured the publication of four hardback books. Granted the Snowmites were nowhere near what they eventually became, but they were still a very fashionable concept that was signed to become a

## The Fairy Tale

Licensing Product in the manufacturing of soft toys and other products, cited as being the next big children's concept; following on with the same success as the *Care Bears* and *My Little Pony*; estimated to create a revenue income of over twenty million pounds in Licensing over a three-year period in UK sales alone.

I began appearing on television programmes and being constantly interviewed for radio and newspaper articles. I also started visiting Primary schools for Story time sessions on a UK tour, which went towards raising money for the UK's Childline charity organisation. It was a dream come true, and I loved every minute of my new-found career.

At the same time, I'd also taken on the role of *'Santa's Secretary'*, answering on average over 20,000 letters a year from children who had written to Father Christmas. The Santa Claus Service was a family tradition on my Father's side of the family. It was started back in the 1930s by my late Grandfather, James Gilmour Senior. Every Christmas Eve he would dress up as Santa Claus and push a hand cart down the cobble streets of Liverpool, giving out presents to the underprivileged children in his neighbourhood.

Then in the 1960s his son, my late uncle James Gilmour Junior, took over the Santa Service and he began weaving his own Christmas magic with a Santa Letter Service. In the run-up to Christmas he donned the famous red suit and put pen to paper, sending every child who wrote to Father Christmas a free personal reply from the great bearded man. He even started a *Dial-a-Santa service* in which children could telephone him and speak directly to Santa Claus.

For my part in the family tradition, I was limited in what I could do. I didn't have my Uncle Jim's deep velvety voice that excited a mesmerized child on the other end of the telephone, and my female appearance didn't create a convincing Santa Claus look.

Uncle Jim mulled over the problem, and within a matter of minutes he had found the solution.

"*I know who you can be*," he announced cheerfully, the sparkling glint of excitement returning to his eyes. "*You can be my Secretary!*"

At first, I wasn't over-enthusiastic at the thought of just being a Secretary. It seemed so ordinary in such a beautiful world of magic, but I should have known better. My Uncle Jim did not do ordinary.

"*You'll make an absolutely wonderful Elf!*" he grinned, sketching out his vision of the new me with custom-made pointed ears, and dressed in a green costume complete with yellow bobbles and silver bells. And that was the beginning of my role as Santa's Secretary - the strict and extremely bossy *Elf Pipkin*.

Even though I was unhappy in my marriage to David, and terrified of my ADEs, I had a life, a physical reality that promised success. The constant sadness I felt at not being able to talk openly about my ADEs and Jesus was hidden behind my smile. I wanted to share with the world my ADEs, and the Snowmites was the only way I could think of doing it.

## The Fairy Tale

It was the only way I could do it - and it would have continued if it hadn't been for that horrible faithful day when I was separated from my children and made homeless, loosing everything. As I vanished from life itself, my publishing contract signed in 1991 became void. It wasn't until 2009 when my publishing dream finally became a reality, and I celbrated the publication of my first Snowmite book, *Island of Ice and The Snowmites* under my pen name *Gilmory James*.

It is indeed in many ways a very sad story. But the fact that this book has now been written shows just how powerful Love truly is. I had my children's love, and I knew Jesus loved me. I held onto my faith with all my might, and as a result the story of Jesus and His journey of my Spirit has now been told. People may have given up on me but Jesus never did.

This book is the beginning of mankind's Higher Consciousness being opened. Evolution and a new path of our survival. The story of how Jesus has visited man, and for the first time in 2000 years lifted the veil of mystery surrounding the book of Revelation. A way forward for us finally to learn how to live in peace with one another.

But it is not just a new Spiritual awakening that has been granted to us. In finally being able to understand the consciousness and its origin, the world of Science can now finally be truly combined with Spirituality. We can at long last grow together in both the Spirit and the physical Mind.

The one main aspect of Actual Death Experiences

that has baffled the medical fields from the onset is the fact that when a subject has an ADE, and experiences the physical death, their brain cells remain undamaged.

Usually, once death is confirmed, the brain cells begin to deteriorate and perish. But millions of people have reported having an ADE, and in every case the brain cells of the subject remain intact during the physical death.

I have a theory that might suggest a reason for this preservation, (and this is not based on Jesus' *Who Am I? Teachings of my Spirit*).

Recently, I stumbled upon the work of an incredible University Professor. His name is Dr. Sean B Carroll, of the University of Wisconsin, Madison, USA.

Dr. Carroll has been studying the DNA of the fruit fly. He discovered that two of the same species of the fruit fly had different appearances. He found one fly had spots on its wing, which the other fly did not have.

In the DNA of the flies, he found the presence of a *switch*. In the fly with the spots, this switch was turned on, whereas it wasn't within the fly without the spots. He then extracted the switch DNA from the spotted fly and injected it into the clear-winged fly. Moments later the clear-winged fly produced spots.

The hypothesis I now offer is that perhaps an ADE subject has a similar type of switch which is turned on, and therefore it preserves the brain cells for a longer period of time after the physical death. Indeed, the answer to the question asked by the Science world may in fact be found in human DNA.

If this premise is proved to be correct, we may have stumbled upon a source of DNA that can be cultivated to treat all known medical ailments due to cell deterioration.

In bringing the Actual Death Experience into the mindset of individuals who have not had an ADE, we can learn to combine Science with Spirituality to lay down the foundations of a society no longer scarred by the rule of violence and war.

The Spirit, while still within the physical body, communicates by means of telepathy. In the *Who Am I? Prophecies of Jesus*, He teaches us how to cultivate our telepathic source so we may begin our next stage of human evolution.

Imagine a world in which we are able to communicate with one another by means of telepathic thought! War would become absolved. State Leaders and Soldiers alike would be able to communicate with one another directly to resolve issues of debate.

Crime rates would plummet as criminals acknowledge there is no longer the reality of the unsuspecting victim. In understanding the Spirit now within our physical lives, the ability to make great changes will be our reward.

Firstly we will need to create an international platform, where everyone, whether science-minded or spiritual-minded, can meet to discuss the Actual Death

Experience in great detail. A forum where ADE subjects can freely give an account of their ADEs, and at the same time explore the aspects of their consciousness in an environment of acceptance and the desire to be educated.

The publication of this book will see the launch of the Human Consciousness Scientific Observational Universal Learning (SOUL) Project. The intent is to create a Collective Consciousness for the study of the ADE in a combination of Science and Spirituality.

The worldwide internet has given us the ability to transfer information between individuals of all backgrounds: the believer and the non-believer, the Scientist and the Spiritualist, and even individuals who are yet to discover what they want to believe in.

The *HC-Soul Project* aims to give everyone the opportunity to ask questions and seek the answers in the publishing of an 'open debate' for the collective consciousness.

The *Who Am I?* Spiritual Prophecies of Jesus teach us that the Human Consciousness is the Spiritual Entity of Man. As such, His teachings change everything we thought we knew in our scientific understanding of the consciousness.

As for myself in my life as a woman, the Spiritual Writings did reveal a future in which I would one day find my own personal and long-awaited happy ending. One day I will meet my life partner - my Soul mate. And when I do, we will have our very own Happily Ever After story........... The End

## Conclusion

*Who be He: My King?*

*He came within the night*
*Wore not a crown of gold*
*To flash before the eye*
*But still*
*I saw the King in Him*
*In his spoken words*
*The breath of wisdom*
*How he knew - his chosen thought*
*Within the silence of Destiny.*

*I pray thou remain with trust*
*To believe in thy Soul*
*I permit not change in the mind of Man*
*Until the truth is told.*

*What sadness became of their rains*
*When the Kings without a Crown*
*Stood to believe*
*The Man of weakness*
*Before me.*

*The sad Kings stand*
*In their Kingdoms of darkness*
*May the breath of thy wind*
*In thy wisdom be strong*
*To blow the clouds away*
*From the Heavens of the Kingdoms*
*Of the sad Kings today.*

*To my King, I will speak the secret*
*For the Tree of the Gold Keys*
*To Him - This Man*
*Who stood to believe in Me*
*For upon the Tree of many Hearts*
*Children are more than one.*

*Here three Hearts have been waiting*
*Within the Fairy Tale*
*To glimmer in Love and Promise*
*Only be he, the name of my King*
*Be not yet engraved upon the Gold*
*For Man's eye to see.*

# Conclusion

# 11

# Conclusion

Many people have often asked me why do I call my experiences Actual Death Experiences rather than Near Death Experiences when they are both of the same phenomenon? It is a personal preference to me, and one that I find identifies the experience with a more suitable term; especially in today's scientific interest in the phenomenon.

Dr Raymond Moody's revolutionary work in 1975 brought the Near Death Experience into the public domain, and his constant work since has seen the public's interest continuingly peak. There is no doubt in my mind that Dr Moody should be applauded for his work, and recognised as a pioneering founder of research into the phenomenon.

However in my opinion, in more recent times Dr Moody's work has been advanced by the research of Dr Sam Parnia who I feel has opened the door for the science world to investigate the phenomenon in a way that can help us to achieve understanding in the combination of science and Spiritually, to help provide the answers to how our Spirituality can improve our physical well-being.

I also feel the term Near Death Experience is now

## Conclusion

often used loosely to describe an incident in which an individual has had a serious accident and he/she almost lost their life, rather than having an actual Spiritual experience.

In my personal opinion, you've had an Actual Death Experience if your heart has stopped beating and your Spirit has risen up out of your physical body regardless of whether you have actually passed through the bright light at the end of the tunnel. Meeting a deceased loved one or another Spiritual being and being sent back is still in my opinion an Actual Death Experience rather than a Near Death Experience.

I can only describe my journey with Jesus as being of a roller coaster ride of emotions as far as my physical life as a woman is concerned. I have felt extreme fear, experienced a tremendous love, held an intense honour, and at times, I also felt an excessive wretchedness but there has also been times of a great laughter.

Every day the different emotions seemed to just roll into each other, and during the period between 1992 and 2012 I would say there was probably not one day that passed when I didn't cry. Sometimes the emotions I felt were so powerful, I would find myself vomiting.

Naturally, I could not let other people see me experience these deep emotions, and other people certainly effected what was happening to me. I knew I was absorbing other peoples energy, and as I absorbed their energy, I would also inherit their emotions. Without any words even needing to be spoken I could feel their sadness, their fears, their disappointments and their hopes but I would feel it in extreme measures.

This is another reason why in many ways I say my children kept me going. The bond between a mother and her child is beyond question the strongest bond we can experience, and the love I held for them kept making me want to be strong - to desire life.

The times when I was simply so exhausted from the physical aspect of having Actual Death Experience, my body constantly aching with pains and experiencing the enduring roller coaster ride of emotions, I would beg Jesus in a normal prayer to just take me and be done with it and not let me come back but my Spirit could not stop loving my children, and in the Actual Death Experiences that love washed over me like the continuing rolling waves of the ocean, making me want to return to my children time and time again.

When my children were younger, I would keep them near to me, always encouraging family activities whenever I felt physically strong enough. We would often turn off the TV and sit around together singing songs or I would tell them stories about the Snowmites, and my children involved themselves in the Dear Santa Letter Service, which I was still doing every year.

At one point I fostered three other children and looked after many more. During one period, I had nine children living with me - all needing care and refuge which I was more than happy to give them, and in return their beautiful innocent hearts where allowing me to live a reasonable normal life as they gave me their energy. I absorbed the children's love and laughter, their hopes and

## Conclusion

dreams and they inexplicable ability to forgive.

Living my life as a woman with a desire to find love in the arms of a man was impossible. It wasn't just because I was having Actual Death Experiences and meeting with Jesus in the Spirit although that alone made a loving physical union with a man unachievable as no man could possibly understand the urgency I felt for Jesus' story to be told, and how exposed I felt, which made a normal relationship seem out of my reach.

I couldn't do the everyday normal activities that one expects from a physical relationship with a partner, - such as going out socializing regularly down at the local pub. I was lucky if I could manage one appearance every few weeks in any social gathering.

Then there was also the aspect in which I would absorb the man's emotions. Whenever I did meet a man, our conversations would always evolve into discussing his emotions, 'Why did he feel the way he did? What was wrong with him? How could he change his life?' and as he explored his emotions with me, he would start to heal himself from all the negativity he was holding inside, and once he was healed, I had to walk away.

No man could have ever understood how physically weak I felt or the beating effect meeting with Jesus in the Spirit was having upon my physical life.

I couldn't be with a man and not share the divine teachings Jesus was teaching me, and for many years I was also too afraid to tell people I was with Jesus in the Spirit. I had to walk away. I had to let the man go. It would have been wrong of me to keep him just because I was lonely and wanted to feel the strength and the protection from the arms of a man and his heart. Everyone deserves to find a true and faithful love with no secrets, and I couldn't give this to a man at the time.

In understanding the relationship between the Spiritual mind and the physical mind, it is very enlightening to realise with courage and an iron rod determination we can all change our lives for the better. Jesus wants us to understand this and through His divine teachings in the *Who Am I? Prophecies* we can come to fully understand the simplicity of the change and transformation of living our lives within a higher state of consciousness.

The positive thought that enriches your Spirit - the core of all your emotions starts with you. The positive thought cannot be created by a third person in your life - you are the creator of the positive thought within your own mind, you generate it, you control it.

Once you make that crucial decision, 'I've had enough of the negative energy around me, I'm going to change' then you will finally see the changes develop within your life. You don't need to suffer a subjugated state of mind. You can free yourself from negative influences, free yourself from the destructive control other people have over your life and become your own person.

In His *Who Am I? Prophecies*, Jesus teaches us to become responsible for our own thoughts and actions. *'Why follow the light of another when we hold the brightest light of all within our own hands - the light of our own love'.*

## Conclusion

He teaches us to respect ourselves by acknowledging responsibility for our own lives.

In life it is very easy to blame another person for a problem. It is much harder to acknowledge blame for our part in how the problem came to be in existence. In understanding that we are indeed in control of our own thoughts we can assess situations more closely to establish true fault. Don't be afraid to ask yourself questions.

*"Am I associating myself with people whose ideas, morals way of thinking are not the same as my own?"*

*"Do I allow other people to make my decisions for me, which I may not agree with?"*

*"Do I remain in the company of people who constantly make me feel bad about myself?"*

If you can answer yes to any of the above questions, then in reality you are bringing conflict into your own life. This conflict will lead to your Spirit feeling rejected, and in thus emanating the sense of confusion, followed by the emotion of sadness for the rejection.

Once you have sensed the emotion of sadness that has been created, you will generate more negative thoughts, and so, it becomes a cycle of destructive thinking. Self doubt, fear, unhappiness are all the threads of destructive thinking. Jesus does not want you to teach these emotions to your Spirit.

When you pass over, it is your Spirit that stands before Jesus. You are presenting yourself before Him with everything you have taught yourself as the *Teacher* within your physical life from the thoughts that you have had.

You no longer have the physical mind, and so, the *Teacher* in you has now gone. You stand before Jesus as the Child of God, your Spirit. When Jesus asks you a question, you have to answer that question as you understand it. You no longer have the ability to decide on what answer you think you should give or what answer you think He wants to hear. The teacher in us had the ability to delegate answers but in the Spirit you dont have that ability.

Jesus becomes your *Teacher*, and His Will is to save you and deliver your Spirit safely into the Kingdom of God. His teachings begin with His *Who Am I?* journey of your Spirit. Jesus wants you to understand who you are as God's creation. God's creation of love, your Spirit, - His Child is pure and beautiful, free from all pain, and a source of powerful positive energy.

Before your conception God did not create your Spirit, His Child to be self indulgent, bossy, as a liar or a murderer. God did not create your Spirit, His Child to feel unworthy and dislike yourself, to doubt, to argue, to lack trust, and all the other bad characteristics that we can teach ourselves.

The truth of God is how God first created you. In Jesus' *Who Am I?* journey of your Spirit, Jesus becomes your *Teacher* to teach you the truth of God for that of His creation of your Spirit. His creation of you in your purest form.

## Conclusion

It is very easy to say and even believe, "I am without sin". To live your physical life without harming another living person. But have you also taken into account the truth of your own thoughts?

It is easy to attend Church everyday or every week and profess love for God. But after you have left the Church service, have you ever engaged in a conversation where you have spoken ill of another person. Have you ever stood conversing with another person, smiling and verbally agreeing with their spoken words but secretly within your thoughts been thinking, 'I wish you'd just go away, you're such a stupid horrible person, how long do I have to stay and listen to this?' or 'I'd better not say what I'm truly thinking.' These thoughts are teaching your Spirit, the Child of God to be judgemental, to be sly, to be untruthful, to desire harm against another'. This negative energy is not of God's love.

When I first met Jesus within an Actual Death Experience, I knew who He was. I recognised His presence by His majestic aura, yet still my Spirit asked of Him,
*"Are you my Lord Jesus?"*

I asked Him a question when I knew the answer. He replied, *"Why do you ask Child do you not know?"*

To understand why I had actually asked Him this question, Jesus had to teach me the truth of my love. In such, although I had loved Him ever since I was a young child, I had never truly opened my heart to Him.

In my younger days when I use to pray to Him. I

would close my eyes and sit us both under a tree and there I would talk to Him about all the things going on in my life, and in the world.

Never once within my thoughts did I allow Jesus to speak back to me. It didn't seem right because this was my way of praying to Him. I didn't know my belief was just an excuse. The real reason I wouldn't allow Him to speak back to me was because I did not feel worthy enough of His words. My own lack of confidence was teaching my Spirit to reject Him.

It was the same lack of understanding that allowed my Spirit to believe it was right to save the Spirit of Trevor Enstone within the *Swallowed By The Mouth of Darkness* Actual Death Experience. After his Spirit was swallowed up by the darkness, I reached down and grasped hold of his hand then called out, "*Don't worry Trevor I will save you*". I then began pulling as hard as I could while reciting the Lord's Prayer. I knew the darkness had no power over the light of God, and so, it could not devour my Spirit.

I did not understand at the time that Trevor Enstone's Spirit was not mine to save. His salvation was for him to find through Jesus. To understand why I had actually believed I could do such, Jesus had to teach me the truth of my love, and He showed me when I first sowed the seed that made me feel I was only happy when I was saving others.

In my teenage years, I use to imagine in the escapism of one's own imagination that I'd done something heroic. I'd save a child in a runaway pram

## Conclusion

from oncoming danger, and as a result everyone around me would see what I had done, and be happy with me for being so brave.

It may appear to be a harmless overzealous teenager's imagination but the truth for why I was conjuring up such an imaginary escapism was because in my reality, I wasn't happy, I didn't have any self confidence. I felt I was living my life in the background of other people's busy and more rewarding lives.

This flaw in my character became quite harmful to me in my adult years, especially when I first became successful in my writing career.

I was governed by a need to save other people. I adopted the attitude that if I could succeed then so too could everyone else who perhaps didn't have the same confidence that I did. What I didn't realise at the time was the confidence I thought I had in myself wasn't a true confidence, it was just a mask of pretence to how I was truly feeling about myself, and so the truth for why I was wanting other people to succeed wasn't truly to improve their lives, it was so I could feel good about myself.

It was a hard lesson to learn, and when Jesus took me upon His *Who Am I?* journey of my Spirit, and showed me the truth, it was difficult to acknowledge my selfishness.

We have to acknowledge that there are indeed people in the world who don't want to be saved, and our part in wanting to save others has to be done from a pure heart.

We should always try and help other's find salvation in Jesus. We should naturally want this for everyone. But we should not do it just to make ourselves feel better. We should do it freely - honestly and without a selfish desire.

This book is not a translation of the New Testaments, and some readers may even be disappointed and claim they could not find Jesus upon these pages. This book is about introducing you to the encounters I've had with Jesus within my Actual Death Experiences.

It is about revealing to you how we all come to stand before Him after we have passed over and how we then begin a one to one journey with Him to be taught the truth of God.

It is about how Jesus is our salvation, and how He has for the first time in two thousand years revealed to mankind His new divine teachings to help us prepare ourselves for Him. The same divine teachings that show us the way to live our physical lives in peace and how we can heal this world that we live in. It reveals how we will evolve into a new state of living by entering into a higher consciousness of existence.

This book is also about how we can combined science and Spirituality as a way forward. How understanding the Spiritual mind now within our physical existence can improve our well-being.

This book is not a print run of the actual *Who Am I? Prophecies of Jesus*. Although, I penned those pages the writing style isn't the usual reading text. They are Spiritual

## Conclusion

writings that proclaim Christ as the Son of God and Saviour of mankind, and Almighty God as our Heavenly Father.

Bible scholars and Ministers alike will most certainly understand the text in the *Who Am I? Prophecies of Jesus*. The style of text being on the same style as biblical verse. The study of these Spiritual Writings will not only give answers to the bibical scholar but they also show the medical fields how the three levels of consciousness interact with each other.

This book is about how Jesus' has given mankind the gift of healing and knowledge. His new divine teachings are not for a society, a world that existed two thousand years ago. They are for today. They are aimed at our society now - the world we live in within the 21st century.

With the worldwide internet being a source of communication, an *international debate* will formulate a conscious state of deliberation provoking questions about the *Who Am I? Prophecies of Jesus* in our modern world.

Can you imagine the change that could come about? State Leaders who publically believe in Jesus will have to reassess their position on their policies regarding war and sending soldiers into foreign territories. Country's that still practice the death penalty will have to reconsider their state laws.

Jesus' presence in bringing His *Who Am I? Prophecies* within our lives today is the only authority that can bring about a massive world change of consciousness within hours of its confirmation.

It will be swift, and touch every corner of the world. No other world leader or several leaders united together could ever achieve the same level of social change in such a  dramatic short space of time...

# Appendix

## 258
### New Elite Characters

### Creating an Innovative Structure

*The Book - Island of Ice and The Snowmites*

## BACK STORY

Zandeer, the Beautiful Spirit of Children is one of the seven Spirit's of the Spirit Council whom come from the celestial Kingdom of Heavenina, inhabited by the people known as the *Spirit's of Love*. The Spirit Council are *Nymous, the Spirit Lord, Gallius the Wise Spirit of the Galaxies, Zelpha, Protecting Spirit of Animals, Zeprus, Noble Spirit of the Oceans, Gadamar, Gentle Spirit of Nature, and Perilon, the Spirit-Wizard,* and their charge is to protect the *Mysterious Crystal of Life,* which bestows the source of life to the people of Heavenina.

On discovering that Perilon intends to take the Mysterious Crystal of Life as his own, giving him the power to open 'the *Pathway of Time*' between Heavenina and earth, which will then permit him to rule over the entire Universe. The Spirit Council banishes Perilon from Heavenina. Enraged by the banishment, Perilon warns the Spirit Council that one day he will come to rule the Universe. To protect the Mysterious Crystal of Life from Perilon, the Spirit Council leave Heavenina, and journey with the Crystal as it drifts through Space.

In a bid to succeed; Perilon creates a freak storm within the heavens to destroy the Spirit Council but his electrifying bolt of lightning hits the Crystal of Life shattering it into six pieces; five of these pieces zoom off at a tremendous speed into the Universe. Nymous, the Spirit-Lord instructs the Spirit Council to go in search for the missing pieces of the Crystal. When each one them has found one of the missing pieces of the Mysterious

Appendix

Crystal; they must remain with it and protect it from Perilon until they have found a Guardian for the Crystal. Then they will be released from their charge and can return back to their home in the heavens.

## THE STORYLINE

Zandeer is the first to find one of the missing Crystal pieces. She discovers it on a deserted iceberg. Then after transforming the bleak iceberg into an enchanting *Island of Ice;* the beautiful Spirit creates the lovable Snowmites: *Aqua, Turquo, Fluo, Gyp, Topaz, Jasper and Jadea.* Each of the Snowmites are named after a precious gem/crystal which is the same colour as their independent body of fur. [To keep an educational content within the realms of fantasy storytelling]. IE.: *Aqua is Aquamarine. Turquo is Turquoise. Gyp is Gypsum. Jadea is Jade. Fluo is Fluorite. Jasper is Jasper, and Topaz is Topaz.*

Zandeer teaches the Snowmites all about the *real children* living on the planet earth, and tells them that they will be able to visit the children through their *Magic Dreams.*

## THE ANIMATED SHORTS and BOOKS

1] Island of Ice and The Snowmites
2] Arrival of The Guardian
3] Crystal Forest
4] Tabasheer, the Magical Crystal Boat
5] The Ice-Wizards Secret Treasure – *[Introducing: Pengy Penguin]*

6] The Snow-Wizards Blunders – *[Introducing: Jewels, the Husky Puppy]*
7] The Rain-Wizard's Rain Storm – *[Introducing: Nim, Bo and Stratus – The Raincloudsmen]*
8] Bobea the Lost Seal
9] The Haunted Forest – *[Introducing: Ice-Worm Wormy]*
10] Gyp's Brave Adventure – *[Introducing: Scutter, Smitter and Scrapper – The Terrible Crystal Creepers]*
11] Jasper's Sledge
12] A Snowy Hill – *[Introducing: Glacia the Polar Bear]*
13] Giant on the Magical Iceberg
14] Santa's Ride

**FEATURING FOUR FOLLOW-ON CONCEPTS**
*Connected together through The Spirit Council and The Mysterious Crystal of Life*

(1) THE STARMITES: 14 Book Titles and Animated Television Shorts. [Accompanying Feature Film – *'Snowmite Magic.'*

Gallius finds a piece of the Mysterious Crystal upon a lone star. He enhances its radiance and it becomes the brightest star in the Galaxies, [the North Star] then Gallius creates The Starmites; naming each Starmite after a birth sign of the Zodiac. The educational content in The Starmites concept includes aspects of the weather, constellation of stars, the Northern Lights and the solar system – ect.

(2) THE ANIMITES: 14 Book Titles and Animated

## Appendix

Television Shorts. [Accompanying Feature Film – *'Snowmite Magic.'*

Zelpha finds one of the missing Crystal pieces in uncharted wilds of an African jungle and there she creates The Animites; naming each of her furry friends after wild animals and aspects of the wilderness.

(3) THE SEAMITES: 14 Book Titles and Animated Television Shorts. [Accompanying Feature Film – *'Snowmite Magic.'*

Down in the depths of the enigmatic vast ocean waters; oblique behind lost sunken treasures, Zeprus, Noble Spirit of Oceans discovers a missing piece of the Mysterious Crystal of Life. Zeprus then creates the Seamites.

(4) THE NATUREMITES: 14 Book Titles and Animated Television Shorts. [Accompanying Feature Film – *'Snowmite Magic.'*

After searching every Rain-Forest known to her: Gadamar the gentle Spirit of Nature ultimately claims the last missing piece of the Crystal, and in the opulence of the searing tropical rain forest she creates The Naturemites.

A Journey of Actual Death Experiences

## THE FULL LENGTH FEATURE FILMS
*Featuring Cesar - the true Guardian of the Mysterious Crystal of Life*

### Running Order 1 - Story Order 2.
*Cesar - The Spiritual Son.*

In the Battle of the Spirit's Legend Cesar must first embrace his Spiritual Destiny before he can begin the rescue for *Pytheas*. Then within the forest of Kobold; he discovers the great Oak Tree and the secret passageway to a world untold in the land of long forgotten legends. Cesar has to choose whom he should rescue between Pytheas and Zandeer, the Beautiful Spirit of Children. The only way, Cesar can rescue them both is for him to be victorious in a battle against Perilon, the Spirit-Wizard.

### Running Order 2 - Story Order 1.
*Merlin's Dream - The Prophecy.*

*Where it began ......*

Before *Merlin* - the Great Wizard of All Ages takes flight upon the mystical winged horse *Pegasus*; by favour of *Zeus*, he seeks out Talisman; Elder of Ozella.

Merlin reveals to Talisman through the flames of destiny; the path of mankind that is already imprinted upon the rock of paved. Merlin shares his visions of mans future with Talisman, warning him about Perilon, the Spirit-Wizard who in trickery and betrayal of the ancient Gods will send down to earth a *Light of Illusion*, promising all who entered the light will be granted magical powers,

Appendix

in thus beginning the birth of the mortal wizard whom will travel far and wide across the world and Europe; setting the scene for all known urban myths.

Unbeknown to to those who took on the magical powers when they had entered Perilon's Light of Illusion, Perilon had taken their Spirits - sucking them up through the Light and holding them captured beneath his *Pyramid of Magic* within the land of Heavenina.

Thus only their soulless physical bodies roamed the earth, while their Spirits are trained to become Perilon's army - *The Thaumic Warlocks* in preparation for Perilon's rule of the universe.

In time Perilon recalls the soulless bodies of the wizards, and they answer the calling as the screaming banshees. He then returns their Spirit's back into their bodies creating hence his army of The Thaumic Warlocks. Great battles of magic then ravaged the lands of earth between the Thaumic Warlocks and the White Wizards.

Talisman, horrified by the visions; fears these unnatural conflicts will bring about the end of civilization. Merlin reassures Talisman; mankind can survive, and makes a promise in prophecy that he will send forth his Spiritual Son whose destiny is to defeat Perilon and his army.

Talisman accepts Merlin's charge to stand as the keeper of Merlin's Spiritual Son. The one who will come at the beginning of the 21st century. Merlin surrenders to Talisman, *'the Ring of Excalibur,'* as only the ring can unveil the identity of the chosen one.

### Running Order 3 - Story Order 3.
*Galaxies Beyond.*

Cesar finds himself caught up within the strange forces of the cosmos He is taken on a journey to explore the wondrous distant stars. There within the phenomenal sector of outer space; Cesar joins Gallius, Wise Spirit of Galaxies in constellation conflict against Perilon, the Spirit-Wizard, [Gallius, creator of The Starmites].

### Running Order 4 - Story Order 4.
*Animal Kingdom.*

Cesar's crusade takes him to the lands of a great African Jungle: Caesar clashes against Perilon to aid Zelpha; Protecting Spirit of Animals,: [creator of The Animites].

### Running Order 5 - Story Order 5.
*The Rising of Atlantis*

Cesar's search takes him to the bottom of the deepest Ocean and Cesar comes to the aid of Zeprus the Noble Spirit of Oceans, [creator of The Seamites] in battle against Perilon.

### Running Order 6 - Story Order 6.
*The Celestial Order.*

Cesar's future takes him into a world within the past: To be mortal or immortal?

Appendix

## Running Order 7 - Story Order 7.
*Miracle of Nature - The New Earth.*

Cesar on discovering a parallel Earth. He passes through the four doorways of the Magic Lands to rescue the people from Perilon and his army of Thaumic Warlocks.

In the final battle; Cesar conquers over Perilon, and the Thaumic Warlocks, aiding Gadamar the Gentle Spirit of Nature, [creator of the Naturemites]. As Perilon falls to his ultimate doom; a great spectacular fête of nature occurs in which the two earth's become as one again.

## Cesar The Spiritual Son

The most ingenious aspect of all the feature films surrounding the character Cesar is that the hero of the story is not actually Cesar as in his life of a young man.

Set in the 21st Century, (With the exception of *Merlin's Dream - The Prophecy*) - Cesar has a rare medical condition that mirrors my own - chronic Actual-Death Experiences, and it is his Spirit whom is applauded as the hero of the story.

In essence Cesar within his physical life faces the challenges of extreme emotions - experiencing confusion, fear, doubt, joy, excitement and also rejection by those he loves, while at the same time his Spirit is destined to adventuring the unknown universe.

## Author's Note

...The Fairy Tale, '*The Tree of The Gold Keys and The White Rose Princess*' that Jesus brought me within my Actual-Death Experiences in 1992 wasn't as I had created within my imagination when I was a child.

As a child it had just been a Once Upon a Time and the Happy Ever After story.

The Tree of the Gold Keys Fairy Tale was to play a very important aspect within my ADEs, as it came to be featured within the *Who Am I?* Stage Play that had been created within my ADEs to tell the story of the Revelations 11, 12, and 13 to begin a time of momentous celebrations honouring the Spiritual Intervention of Jesus upon humanity.

Appendix

## The Fairy Tale

## *The Tree of The Gold Keys and The White Rose Princess*

Once upon a time in a far away magical Kingdom. There lived a beautiful Princess who had a very special garden. It was a garden of the most beautiful white roses one had ever seen, and to the Princess it was a place of the heart because she believed the white rose was the rose of true love.

Now across from the white rose garden, there was a mysterious island surrounded by water, and in the middle of the island there was a large oak tree with tiny gold keys hanging down from its branches. The tiny gold keys would tinkle softly together, creating sweet melodies which were then carried away by the gentle wind.

As with all things that are mysterious. There was a story about the Tree of the Gold Keys that was believed by all the people who lived in the magical Kingdom, and beyond. It was a legend in which they told to their children and their children's children, and to every passing traveller who came to the Kingdom.

It was a story of a Spirit who lived upon the island

guarding the Tree of the Gold Keys. The Spirit was known to all as the Spirit of Love, and it was believed that if a man seeking out his true love sat underneath the oak tree, then the tiny gold keys would sing softly the song of his heart, which could only be heard by his one true love.

One day, the beautiful Princess was sitting in her garden when she looked across at the island, and there she saw a very handsome stranger sitting all alone underneath the Tree of the Gold Keys. He was watching his reflection dance upon the rippling waves of the water.

Now for many days and many nights, the Princess sat in her garden watching her stranger and with each new passing day she fell deeper and deeper in love with him. Then early one evening just as the sun was setting, the Princess suddenly began to hear a beautiful melody within the wind and she knew deep within her heart that the tiny gold keys were whispering to her the song of her handsome stranger's heart. Only as she listened ever so carefully, she realized with a great sorrow that it was a very sad song,

*'Oh how unhappy his heart must be,'* thought the Princess sadly, and she wondered what could have happened to her handsome stranger to make him feel so sad.

Suddenly, the Princess began to feel very sleepy. She closed her eyes and then fell into a deep sleep, and in her dream she saw a single tiny gold key.

When the beautiful Princess woke up from her dream; she

Appendix

saw the Lord of Dreams standing beside her and she heard him speak softly to her,

*"My dear sweet White Rose Princess. You have seen the gold key to your stranger's heart and so within your heart your love for him is true. Close your eyes once more, and I will send you the Spirit of Love who will take you across to the island."*

The beautiful Princess did as the Lord of Dreams had told her, and when she opened her eyes again she saw the Spirit of Love waiting down by the water's edge on a large wooden craft.

The White Rose Princess stood up and walked down to the water's edge and stepped onto the wooden craft, and the Spirit of Love silently rowed her across to the island where she met with her handsome stranger. Then the Spirit of Love disappeared, leaving the Princess and her handsome stranger to be alone together.

There they sat underneath the Tree of the Gold Keys talking all about their hopes and wishes, until eventually their words became words of love for each other. But unbeknown to the beautiful Princess; her handsome stranger had not spoken the truth when he had talked of his life to her, and this was now making him feel very sad indeed.

He had fallen deeply in love with the Princess, and he knew deep down inside his heart he would have to tell her the truth about his life. Only now, he was afraid that she would not love him for the man he truly was. He had told the Princess that he was just a mere kitchen boy of no wealth, who worked in the palace kitchens of a great King from another Kingdom. But in truth, he had been wandering the lands for many months seeking out the Tree of the Gold Keys after his heart had been broken by a fine lady, who had only loved him for his land and for his wealth; for he was truly a Prince, the son of a King.

With deep sorrow in his heart for speaking such a terrible lie to the beautiful White Rose Princess, his voice trembled as he asked her,

*"You are a Princess of royal blood, do you not desire to marry only a Prince?"*

The Princess shook her head and smiled, as she looked deep into his eyes,

*"I do not search for a Prince,"* she told him. *"I seek only a King, and you my dear kitchen boy is he, for only a true King can pull a sword from the stone."*

Now the handsome Prince did not understand her words, and so the Princess explained,

*"Before I met you my dear King,"* the Princess began. *"My heart had been broken by a very cruel Prince, and so wounding was his deed of betrayal, my heart had ached until eventually it became as cold as stone without any feelings. But you have now brought warmth back into my heart."*

The handsome Prince took the Princess in his arms and held her tightly. He knew it did not matter whether he was a Prince or a pauper, for he had finally found his one and only true love.

Appendix

Then as they both closed their eyes, their dreams became one.

In the nights that followed they shared the same dreams, and as their love for each other grew; their Spirits joined together and danced through the night, rising up into the evening clouds to be blessed by the Spirit of Love.

Then together in the Spirit they made a child, and when their child in Spirit came forward. The Lord of Dreams appeared, and took their child to live in the clouds of the mysterious heavens, to teach him of the future.

While in the light of the day the beautiful White Rose Princess and her handsome King came together in their truth, and built themselves a strong bridge in which they walked across into the white rose garden.

The garden of true love. And they both lived happily ever after.

The End .........

# References

Moody Raymond Dr. Ph. D., Ms.D.,                page 15
Parnia Sam Dr. M.D., Ph.D., M.R.C.P.            page 16

**Biblical Reference:**
1 Corinthians (6:19)                             page 58
2Corinthians (12: 1-9)                           page 15
Jesus. Light of the World (John 8:12)            page 34
John the Apostle: Book of Revelation (21:10)     page 15
Matthew 6 (14-15)                                page 74

# Book Reviews

### Roger Rowlands CBT Psychotherapist

'The detailed accounts and experiences are sympathetically reflected with self-compassion and a spiritual empathy, demonstrating a deeper understanding of the phenomenon. I have experienced with other patients NDE's; which are more often linked to 'actual near physical death' experiences; usually following a severe road accident collision and subsequent physical injuries; however the Author's particular experiences, are unusual and acquired through her consciousness senses; with a longevity of thirty years, which from my limited knowledge is quite unique.

I feel the reader with a curiosity for life and afterwards, will find this a fascinating, enjoyable and heartfelt book, which does stir the question of, how we can combine science and spirituality in the future?

### Amanda Stable

I wasn't sure what to expect when I first started reading this book. I have really enjoyed the science and real life combination. The book is a fascinating insight into the

Afterlife, and the author's Actual Death Experiences. Every ADE she has, appears to set out a lesson of greater knowledge obtained by the author meeting with Jesus within the Afterlife.

Some people may find it hard to believe what the author goes through during her ADEs, and to them, I say *'read this book.'* The author has been through many difficult times to get where she is today. She has faced so much negativity from people around her, including friends and family. She has had to fight with Health Authorities and Social Services professionals just to have her ADEs acknowledge.

Within this book, there are a collection of the Author's Actual Death Experiences. These are amazing to read and I'm thrilled the author has decided to share them with the world. They are all so interesting, I wish she had shared more.

This book has helped me to realise that I should not be afraid of death, that death is not the end. Death is just another journey of our lives.